AF326660

About Our Featured Author

Kirk Horan has dedicated his life to service, joining the Coast Guard at age 18 and spending 20 years as a firefighter. Now he focuses on building leaders.

While recovering from an injury as a full-time firefighter, Kirk began his network marketing journey in 2009, reaching financial success in his thirties. He earned multiple accolades, including the highest award his company offered, and was honored with several magazine features and a cover story in *Success from Home*. Kirk reached a defining moment when he attained the top rank in the company while still balancing a full-time job as a firefighter.

In 2022, he transitioned to a new energy-focused network marketing company. The ground-floor opportunity reignited his drive, and he soon led one of the fastest-growing teams in the organization. He and his wife Trisha travel the country in their motor coach, building leaders and expanding their reach.

When not traveling for business or pleasure, Kirk and Trisha spend their time in Florida and the Northeast.

Praise

"Kirk is a super-tenacious leader; every time situations in life have knocked him down, he gets back up and comes back stronger than ever. He has a laser focus to continually grow and produce his desired end results, not just for himself, but for all the people he leads. He is a leader who truly cares about his teams and leads by example, embodying the principle that people will do what you do, not what you say."

—Carlos Marin, Founder and CEO, Lifepower LLC

"There are few people who combine these three elements when it comes to success: (1) They've actually done the hard work and succeeded, (2) They have succeeded at a high level for a sustained period of time, and (3) They have kept their morals, values, and integrity in place as they succeeded. Kirk Horan is one of those rare people who has done all three."

—Justin Prince, Entrepreneur, International Speaker, Author

"I have watched and worked with Kirk Horan as he went from beginner in the industry and a great student to a great leader in his own right as he leads masses of entrepreneurs, mentoring future leaders in how to give more, realizing that it is only through lifting up others that you achieve greatness. Kirk has done so and over the years has become a leader's leader!

Kirk came from a non-business background, and through hard work and study under the guidance of other leaders, he has reached the top of the MLM industry. When you have the opportunity to train or work with Kirk's mentorship, do not let it pass you by. His leadership is the result of being coachable and teachable as he puts in the work to help others reach their dream. I am very proud of what Kirk Horan has achieved and marvel at watching his continued growth and success."

    —Steve Thompson, "Never Quit Steve," best-selling author of *View From the Top and What it Really Takes to Get There; A* Top Earner in the Network Marketing Industry.
Get Excited, Stay Focused and Never Quit!

STAND ON THE SHOULDERS™

of

MINDSET MASTERY COACHING

GIANTS

FEATURING

13 POWERHOUSE AUTHORS: PROVEN MINDSET MASTERY COACHING AUTHORITIES SHARE THEIR INSPIRING JOURNEYS TO THRIVING AND LIVING AT THE HIGHEST LEVELS POSSIBLE.

Kirk Horan

Johnny Wimbrey

Samuel Bean

Markita Brooks

Curt Havens

Col. Tammy S. Hinskton

Daine Patton

Brenda Petrillo

Candy Pruitt

Cal Quigley IV

Chris Robinette

Carol & Brandon Syler

Jeff Tiegs

Published by Wimbrey Training Systems, 550 Reserve Street, Suite 190 Southlake, Texas 76092

Printed in the United States of America

ISBN 978-1-971010-19-9

Dedication

To my wife, Trisha, and my sons, Justin and Adam—your love, patience, and belief in me gave me the strength to keep going, even when the road was tough.

To my family—thank you for standing behind me with unwavering support.

To my team and mentors—your encouragement and faith fueled this mission from the start.

And to John Pyonteck and Jim, Ed, and Brenden Kenney— your guidance helped me find direction when I needed it most.

This book is proof that if you keep showing up, keep believing, and never give up, anything is possible.

Contents

Introduction

An Introduction to
The Stand on the Shoulders of Giants™ Series

This powerful new hardcover series is inspired by the words Sir Isaac Newton made famous: *If I have seen further, it is by standing on the shoulders of giants.*

The first three books in the series are:

- *Stand on the Shoulders of Multi-Million-Producing Giants*
- *Stand on the Shoulders of Top-Producing Giants*
- *Stand on the Shoulders of Mindset Mastery Coaching Giants*

There was a time in my life when I was expected to fail. By the grace of God, I succeeded because I was able to stand on the shoulders of giants. Now it's my turn to pass on the quantum boost I received. The authors contributing to the *Stand on the Shoulders of Giants* series are modern-day giants and elite leaders, and sharing their knowledge is vital to my life's work.

My guidelines for publishing this extraordinary hardcover series were simple but compelling: I knew it was vital to introduce you to modern giants—men and women of character and authenticity who thrive despite the world of compromise in which we live. The authors aren't perfect. They haven't lived flawless lives, nor have I. But as you turn the pages of each book in the *Stand on the Shoulders of Giants* series, you'll discover the authors' exceptional principles and character, their generosity of spirit, their brilliance. *Their truth.*

Each book in our guaranteed best-selling series is unique, and each author is chosen carefully for their strong story and character. You will find genuine connections and authentic voices that resonate with you.

In today's social media-driven culture, we are witnessing a shift unlike any other in human history. For the first time since the beginning of time, society is elevating people to "giant" stature based on the number of followers they have, the number of views they generate, and how many comments are made on their platforms. We are celebrating *visibility* over *credibility* and confusing *influence* with *wisdom*.

I believe in something much deeper—what every ancient tribe understood instinctively when life gets real: **You don't go to the influencers; you go to the elders.** You go to those who have *lived, fallen, and risen again* and have scars that speak louder than any trending soundbite. You go to the ones who carry wisdom for survival—and who can share and inspire.

These are my giants, my elders, whom I invited to be in this series.

They are elders in their achievements, experience, character, wisdom, and leadership. Though relatively young, they write not from a platform of perfection, but from a foundation of truth. Our authors are qualified at the highest elite levels—because *they've been there; they've done that*. And they excelled.

Now they offer their shoulders to you, to boost you to a better view of your path ahead.

As we know all too well, our paths aren't always smooth. Sir Winston Churchill perfectly captured the heartbeat of the *Stand on the Shoulders of Giants* series when he said:

If you're going through hell, keep going.

Every one of the modern-day giants who authors a chapter in our series keeps going on the path of success—through setbacks, shame, failure, heartbreak, loss, rejection, betrayal, and pressure that would break most people. They don't stop. And because they don't, they have more than just massive success—they have substance and character.

When you connect with modern giants and they elevate your thinking, extraordinary things begin to happen. Your mind expands, your options and possibilities broaden, you challenge your limitations, and you start living your life without the limitations that have held you back. You see better and further.

I challenge you: Make a commitment to each title in our powerful *Stand on the Shoulders of Giants* series and find the giants who help you see further. Don't skim the chapters. Don't cherry-pick. Read every story—from front to back. Take your time. Sit with their stories and listen to their voices. Take what they offer and see further down the road.

Awaken the giant within you!

—*Johnny Wimbrey, Ph.D.*

Foreword

'm honored to bring you the third book in the best-selling *On the Shoulders of Giants*™ series. Twelve of the most impressive professionals and business people in the United States and Canada have joined me to write *Stand on the Shoulders of Mindset Mastery Coaching Giants*.

Each of the people who joined me to write a chapter in this book was chosen by me after multiple interviews and my team's careful consideration of what they have to offer you. Every author is a highly sought-after leader, a top-level producer in entrepreneurship or sales, or a visionary, high-performance founder. I know their habits, strengths, and weaknesses.

My co-authors are at different stages of their careers, but you will notice we all have one important thing in common: *We look forward to the future.* We maintain a far-sighted view of our opportunities and possibilities while we build our legacies.

We are elite-level leaders with empire mindsets. We are not limited by our pasts. Without shame or excuses, we share our mistakes, what we're most proud of, and which ethical and moral standards guide us. Many of us talk about our deep faith and how it has helped us. We discuss our attitude, making room for philanthropy, and making the most of second (or third, or fourth) chances. We have much to offer you.

As in all the titles within the *Stand on the Shoulders of Giants* series, our integrity and character are the heart of this powerful book. We realize their importance to our success. This book is about building the character and resilience you need to succeed.

"Standing on the shoulders of giants" is a metaphor almost 1,000 years old; it means having the opportunity to build on the wisdom and truths of others who've gone before you. The genius Isaac Newton made the phrase famous when he wrote, "If I have seen further, it is by standing on the shoulders of giants."

In *Stand on the Shoulders of Top-Producing Industry Giants*, we offer you the unprecedented opportunity to stand on our shoulders, share our wisdom, see your future more clearly, and reach it sooner.

Johnny Wimbrey, Ph.D.

STAND ON THE SHOULDERS™
of
MINDSET MASTERY COACHING

GIANTS

Live Life On Your Own Terms

KIRK HORAN

A car hit me when I was just five years old, and I haven't taken life for granted since. My broken shoulder was just the first in a series of health crises and accidents; each one has strengthened my appreciation of every moment I have. That awareness keeps me determined to live on my own terms.

You keep things in perspective when you're living on borrowed time. In my case, I'm never going to retire and spend my life being idle. I tried it for a year when I first arrived in Florida several years ago—what a waste of my time! I was bored, without purpose, asking my wife, Trisha, for suggestions on what to do, but I couldn't bring myself to work for someone else. I'm an entrepreneur, and I'd only work for myself and my team.

The idea of someone looking over my shoulder and telling me what to do goes against my grain. I've always had a good work ethic, a gift from my stepdad, Dave, the man who raised me. I know how to relax, travel, and enjoy life, too, and I've put together a mix of the two that's perfect for Trisha and me, with plenty of time for family and friends. I truly enjoy helping others.

My entire adult life has been in service to others, whether I was in the Coast Guard, a firefighter in upstate New York, or helping others toward financial freedom in my current business. Being a firefighter had been my dream since I was a little boy, and I made it a reality. As a bonus, I enjoyed my schedule's flexibility. I worked two 10-hour days, two 14-hour nights, followed by four days off. It was a great schedule and allowed me irreplaceable time to do all the other things that enriched my family's life and mine.

I joke, "I thought we were middle class but I'm pretty sure we were poor." My childhood was great, though, and I have no regrets. My three brothers and I lived with Mom and Dave, both of whom we admired and loved. We also had a relationship with my dad, whom we saw on weekends. My parents worked very hard to support us, but they struggled paycheck to paycheck, like at least two-thirds of American families. Yes, we lived in a single-wide trailer, but it felt truly like home to us. I wore a lot of hand-me-downs, but my mom stowed away money to buy us some nice things. When all the kids were wearing Air Jordans, she saved the money and got me a pair. Our borderline poverty didn't traumatize me; it just made me want the finer things in life when I could finally buy them myself.

We four boys were taught to work hard and never give up until we achieved our goals. We had a good lesson on this concept when our well went dry. It had dried up before, but this time we waited days without seeing a drop. When Dave found a dowser to locate an underground vein of water, we kids were doubtful, but my brother Stephen and I started digging by hand. Our equipment was pretty primitive—just two shovels, a rope, and a five-gallon bucket to pull the dirt and clay out of the pit. We dug for 16 feet (though it seemed a mile) before we finally hit enough water to supply our family. We learned a valuable lesson: ***Keep digging.***

I've worked hard since I was 14, and started earning decent money at 16, working weekends for the trucking firm where Dave drove a semi.

I was frugal and saved my earnings, paying cash for big-ticket items. First, I bought an all-terrain vehicle just like every other boy in upstate New York, then I saved for my first car, a 1979 Volkswagen Rabbit.

When I was 17, an accident with a log splitter caused me to almost lose my left hand. Thanks to advice from my uncle, who was a lawyer and a judge, I ended up with a $20,000 financial settlement, a veritable fortune to me. My mother tried to tie it up in a trust until I was 25 and hopefully more mature, but I convinced her I needed the money now. It was more than enough to buy a Monte Carlo and trick it out with great wheels and a few custom touches. Being 17 and stupid, I all too soon blew through the money and then blew the engine. I borrowed Dave's truck until I got out of high school.

The U.S. Coast Guard signed me up for a two-year active-duty tour while I was still in high school. Their boot camp is notoriously tough, second only to the Marines, but my first shock, as it is for many recruits, was the haircut. This was in the late '80s, and of course I had long curly rock-star type hair. Waving his electric clippers, the barber welcomed me, "Have a seat, Bon Jovi!" That first bald stripe right down the middle of my head did exactly what it was meant to do—it got my attention and made me a bit less proud of my well-honed individuality.

I did well, bald or not, and as one of the top seamen apprentices in my boot camp company, I got to choose wherever I would be stationed. Though I'd joined the Coast Guard to see the world, I chose New York City to be close to home. The city was light-years away from upstate New York in every way but geographically.

Every car dealer and credit card company goes after servicemen; I'm sure I had a target on my back. Even before I got to my duty post, I bought a new truck with a good-sized loan. My first use of credit breached some kind of inner barrier, and with few exceptions, my good saving and spending habits went down the tubes and didn't resurface for the next twenty years.

The Coast Guard station was on Governor's Island, a quick ferry ride from the tip of Manhattan, and my workplace was New York Harbor. For two years, my life was exciting. We "Coasties" looked pretty dashing in our uniforms, especially with our 9mm semiautomatic pistols on our hips. Our largest patrol boat was 41 feet long, fast, maneuverable, and a blast to drive. We rescued people, enforced maritime boating laws, fought fires, and did drug busts, backed up by our big guns on deck. One drug bust was for the record books; we seized tons of cocaine bricks packed into metal tubes welded to the hull of a trawler.

As often as possible, I walked around the city, awed by the sheer money that flowed through the whole metropolis. We were welcomed everywhere, even as underage seamen, including just about every bar in the city. On New Year's Eve in Times Square, we'd only have to show our military identification and the police stationed us right under where the ball dropped.

We took every opportunity to learn about other Coast Guard vessels and units. I still cherish a posed photo of me, hanging under a helicopter in a recovery basket with the Statue of Liberty in the background. When my active duty was up, I had a two-year commitment in active reserves, which meant I was just a weekend warrior, stationed in Burlington, Vermont.

1992 wasn't a good year to look for a job. I signed up with a temp agency and took a whole series of short-term and menial jobs while I tried to fulfill my dream of being a firefighter, the job I'd wanted since I was a kid. I changed oil at a quick-lube place, poured concrete foundations, worked as a mason's helper, ran a vending route, and worked at a furniture store on the loading dock. They were all just jobs—whatever I could do to earn money.

My stepfather advised all four of us, "Whatever you do, don't be a truck driver." Of course, that became our goal, and all four of us got our commercial driver's licenses (CDLs). Finally, I was able to make a decent wage, and I enjoyed driving, working 12 hours a day next to my two oldest brothers.

Still, I worked tirelessly to get accepted by the NYC fire department. I thought they were the best of the best, and that's what I wanted to be. Their physical test is tough, but I passed

it with "above average" results and finally was offered a position. When Trisha, then my girlfriend, told me there was no way she'd live in New York City, I turned down the offer; it was already clear that she was *The One.*

In 1996, I accepted a position at my local City of Johnstown Fire Department, and that was one of the best days of my life. When Trish and I were married the next year, I was on top of the world. I was 26 years old, with both the job *and* the woman of my dreams.

Something in my subconscious kept urging me to buy residential rental property, not just a single-family house like every other newly married couple. We had lived in two of three apartments carved out of one large house in town, first the second-floor studio in the back, then the mid-sized apartment in front of it. The landlady's mother lived in the big flat on the ground floor, and we asked the landlady to sell us the building whenever her mother moved out. Not only did she say yes, she offered to carry a private mortgage for ten years. We agreed to her terms and moved downstairs, where we lived for the next few years.

Buying income property was the best financial decision we made as a young couple, and one of the last good ones I made for the next few years. Trish worked, and I had three jobs: the fire department, and on my off days I drove trucks and worked for a roofing business. We thought we had plenty of spending money and got sucked into using credit to buy all the adult toys everyone else was buying—after all, my second and third jobs paid the credit cards and all these extra bills for the toys and goodies. We started to develop a "keeping up with the Joneses" mentality.

Justin was born in 1999; two years later, we bought a nice house in a country setting, on a quiet dead-end street within the city limits, and the next year Adam arrived.

Four days after Adam was born, I learned I had an aortic dissection that turned into an aneurysm, a rupture between layers of the biggest artery in the body. The doctors observed and talked for two months. I explained I wasn't worried about dying as much as losing my job. They listened, and when it was finally time to operate, they performed an unusual surgery by not splitting my sternum down the middle as usually done. If they had, I never could have been a firefighter again. Instead, they cut me up the middle from my belly button to my ribs, then around to the top of my back, an unusual route to the aorta. It was a huge surgery and left a gigantic scar, but it allowed me to recover fully and return to work after a year, which is rare for an aortic aneurysm.

Fortunately, I hadn't used any sick time during my seven years as a firefighter; I had enough sick days in the bank to keep me from missing a check. The bad news was I couldn't do my other jobs, either, and they covered the payments on the car, truck, ATV, snowmobile, furniture, and home improvements. We realized with a shock that the income from our three rental apartments was the only thing keeping us afloat and maintaining our good credit.

My year at home gave me quality time with my sons, and I bonded with them in ways I couldn't do when I was working three jobs. What I didn't realize was that this was the first episode in an every-three-years cycle of health crises and missed work.

In 2003, I was back to work, and in 2006 I fell off a roof. With a concussion and broken wrist, I had four months off. In 2009, I went snowmobiling with my coworkers after a night shift and ran my machine right into a tree at 50 mph (yes, I was always a risk-taker), and that was another four months off. Every time, I had enough sick pay to get me through. Also again, I couldn't drive a truck or do roofing and struggled to pay the bills.

Perhaps I was the cat with nine lives, but we were financially vulnerable, and I didn't like being in debt.

While I was still on leave, I heard about an intriguing energy business from my brother firefighter, and I drove us one-handed through a snowstorm to find out more. Once I arrived, I realized it was network marketing, and I rolled my eyes, but agreed to stay because I'd driven my coworker. Then the more I heard, the more I liked it. This was an energy service program, not selling products, and it really did save people money. That mattered to me.

The initial investment was $450, so whether I liked it or not was moot. We were as broke as we usually were when I was on sick leave. Trisha and I talked, and we didn't see how we could afford the money or the extra time. We were in debt, working four jobs between us, and our sons needed our time and attention. We couldn't stretch ourselves any thinner.

That night I couldn't sleep; my gut feeling told me this was something we shouldn't pass up. I became convinced that this was an important moment in my life and I couldn't blow it. That day I quietly signed up under a firefighter I'd met at the presentation, paying by credit card and not telling Trisha. My first "why" was earning the investment back before she saw the credit card bill.

Because I was still on medical leave, I focused on going from 0 to 60 miles per hour with this new business. Being a skeptic by nature, I called my sponsor many times a day, and soon he kicked me upstairs, giving me direct access to our upline. This was the best gift he could have given me. Now I had access to great mentors, the top leaders in the company. One of them had been on the ground floor, and he was already a millionaire.

From that moment, I made sure I took full advantage of my first-ever mentors. I joined all of the team calls and video meetings—everything that was offered—and made sure my fledgling team took advantage of the information. I took what I learned from the leaders above me and began to develop my own leadership style.

I started off by duplicating what I'd been taught, but with enough replication my in-home meetings and training soon became spontaneous and comfortable. My team knew from the beginning that I truly cared about them and wanted to help them succeed.

Within a year I made more with the energy company than I earned from my two side jobs. I quit them both when I realized how much potential my new business offered and that I should use every spare moment to focus on building it. By the end of my second year, the energy business income surpassed my firefighter salary.

In 2012, I was hurt fighting a structure fire and broke several ribs. This was the fourth time in ten years that I couldn't work, but the first time I didn't worry about finances while on medical leave. We were stable financially, even comfortable, though I wasn't tempted to leave my firefighting job.

Those four months on leave were well spent; I worked the business full-time and made more money than I'd ever earned in any four-month period.

Yes, I cared about the money, but I also cared about the community we were creating in my team, both the camaraderie and the realization we were better than the sum of our parts. From my years in the fire department, I knew it was all about teamwork, caring for and supporting each other, and playing together when we relaxed. We had all kinds of gatherings in my company—beach parties, holiday parties, and of course team-building exercises.

Every aspect of my new career didn't come naturally to me; public speaking was my biggest fear. Before my first big speech to 4,000 people, I was more scared than I'd ever been while running into a burning building. But I was motivated: I was determined to succeed, and we did. I was 37 years old, and not too old to change my mindset. I wasn't stuck in a rigid pattern; I was young and eager to change the way I'd been thinking for the last 20 years.

Trisha and I met many successful people, and I realized they didn't have anything I didn't. Though my success was quick, it seemed comfortable, like a natural progression. Within my first eleven months in the new business, I reached the second-highest possible rank and won a major award.

> "My entire adult life has been of service to others"

Whenever I think back to those early days, I'm still surprised by how hard I pushed myself. I'd work a 10-hour shift, come home, change, drive four hours across the entire length of Massachusetts to Cape Cod where one of my biggest teams was located, give a 45-minute overview, drive four hours home, sleep a few hours, and report in for another shift.

Four years after we began in network marketing, we were comfortable enough for Trisha to quit her job; I like to say I "retired my wife." Three years after that, I retired from the fire department at 45 with twenty years under my belt, the youngest firefighter in that department to ever retire. We didn't buy a bigger house or start spending any wilder; we'd learned our lesson and were thinking about our future.

During a trip to Mexico, Trisha and I had earned, the Chief Executive Officer gave me good advice: *You're going to earn a lot of money; pay your taxes and don't get in over your head.* We took that to heart and began to pay off our mortgage and other debts. This doesn't mean we stopped spending; we just prioritized much better. As the boys were growing up, we didn't hesitate to spend money to make our house as inviting to their friends as possible—a saltwater pool, and a great yard where they could gather and play. I took pride in giving them what my parents couldn't give me when I was growing up.

We also gave them experiences rather than just material things—travel, including overseas trips. We felt these would be adventures to remember and they'd have a better view of the world. I remembered all too well leaving home for the first time on my way to Coast Guard boot camp.

Once we were free and clear, we started to invest. Not all our investments were blue chip, and when we lost $160,000 in something that turned out to be just a scheme, I thought with disbelief, "Who'd have thought we'd lose $160k and it wouldn't wipe us out?"

Above all, we did our best to keep our common sense and our sense of humor. I'd inherited my optimism from my mother, and it came in handy more than once. When things started going really well for us, Trisha reminded me to stay humble and let my results speak for themselves, and I've done my best to live up to her standards.

While I know I have leadership skills, I don't like to only be the face of leadership. I truly like doing the job, too. That became clear when I was up for promotion to captain at the fire department. It was the first time I'd felt the weight of the world on my shoulders, and it slipped off the moment I withdrew my application.

After my 2012 work accident, we had a welcome ten-year stretch when I didn't have a health crisis or accident, but many in my family did. I lost my stepfather, then my mother; Trisha had a benign tumor on her pancreas which called for serious surgery and terrified me. My closest brother, the father of seven children, committed suicide. Our most recent tragedy was losing my son's girlfriend to a head-on collision; she was part of our family. We've had our share of pain.

Our business changed for the worse in 2018 after the company was swallowed up in a corporate buyout and its focus became profits for the shareholders. Top leadership stopped listening to those of us who'd built the company, and I was disappointed that it also pulled out of New York State. I retreated from active leadership, speaking only when I was requested to, and stopped recruiting. It was no longer the valuable service that first attracted me, and I didn't consider it to be a viable opportunity.

The pandemic in 2020 triggered a series of major life changes for us. First, we decided to sell the rental property. It had saved us during the first ten years of our marriage, but with tenant-protection rules in place during the pandemic, it was more of a millstone than an asset. The next year, we realized Justin and Adam were grown up and we asked ourselves whether we still needed our house. It had been a great place to raise our sons, but it had become another millstone. A motor home was far more inviting, and Florida and Cape Cod were beckoning.

In July 2021 the house sold in 48 hours with multiple offers. We'd researched motor homes and tow vehicles, and found one that was perfect, barely used. We parked it on the lawn while we sorted, packed, and stored our belongings. When the boys moved into a rental property, we regretted selling our triplex the year before—but just for a second.

Southwest Florida is ideal for us at this time in our lives. When our sons start raising their families, we plan to spend more time nearby so we can be part of our grandchildren's lives, but for now our motor home and the park model we bought for when we're not traveling fill all our needs.

In 2022, after a few years of just receiving a dwindling but still substantial stream of passive income, I called the energy company and asked to transfer my business to my kids, and I was furious when they stonewalled me and said *no*. I wasn't about to be held hostage and resigned immediately—I just walked away from my residual income. My decision to leave wasn't hard—expensive, yes! But it felt like the right thing to do.

My usual rule is to hold off making a decision for 24 hours. That time I didn't follow my own rule, yet when I said *I resign!*, the weight of the world slid off my shoulders, just as it had when I withdrew from consideration for captain. There are no regrets.

In 2022, I began another, shorter series of health crises. I was planting a palm in my Florida yard and heard a pop when I straightened up. I knew immediately what happened, so I walked into the house and said calmly, "Don't panic, Trisha. I'm going to take a shower and then we're headed to the emergency room. I've got this!" It was another aortic dissection, and serendipitously, I was transferred to a nearby teaching hospital where one of only a dozen doctors in the world performs a special, customized stent insertion to fix the aorta. My poor torso wasn't abused with another few hundred stitches, and I recovered much faster this time.

As I recovered, I realized I was getting up in the morning and facing a day without purpose. Every day at breakfast, I said, "What do you want to do today, babe?" This was not a good place for my brain to be. I was still smarting a bit from my energy company experience, but it seemed I wasn't as turned off as I'd thought. When my friend John called me a dozen times about a start-up company and refused to take *no!* for an answer, gradually I segued from complete disinterest to excitement.

The idea of being part of a start-up, being in on the ground floor—that was intriguing. By November, I was finally ready to travel to Connecticut and meet the corporate team at a prelaunch meeting. Immediately I was all-in. Former teammates, people who believed in me, were scattered across the country, and I began putting my team together.

Our website was activated in January 2023, the same month I went to the ER with a blood clot behind my knee and ended up in surgery yet again. February was our company's launch, so I pulled up a pair of compression socks and John and I hit the road for a month-long corporate road tour: up the east coast, over to Chicago, back and down to Florida, 7,000 miles, shaking hands, greeting our new partners and teammates. From the start, we were one of the fastest-growing teams.

Our new company is exciting, responsive, and the work is fun. It truly offers a valuable service, and I admit without any embarrassment that being in at the beginning has been very rewarding. I had always envied my mentor who'd been in at the start of my first team and was glad to have the opportunity to do that myself. I can truly build something of value and make a difference.

> " I took full advantage of having my first-ever mentors. "

Two months after the launch when New England was beginning to thaw out, we headed north in our motor home for the summer and fall, planning to stay on Cape Cod near my resurrected team and in New York with our sons. We were still on the Cape in November when I realized I had another clot. I recognized the symptoms immediately and knew what needed to be done. I also knew it wasn't going to kill me overnight or in the next couple of days. We packed up and drove down to my vascular surgeon in Florida, and I was completely unsurprised when he said I needed another surgery.

There was one issue: Surgery was weeks away and I'd just earned an all-expense-paid trip to Hawaii. I was determined Trisha wouldn't miss seeing Kauai for the first time; she really deserved it for the unwavering support she'd given me over the last 12 months, and it'd be an auspicious end to the year. I convinced my surgeon to move me to the head of the line.

Though I'm a person who looks forward more than backward, writing this chapter has given me cause to reflect on my choices

ABOUT KIRK HORAN

Kirk Horan has dedicated his life to service. He joined the Coast Guard at age 18 and spent 20 years as a firefighter, a childhood dream he achieved at age 25. Now he focuses on helping people grow, succeed, and become exceptional leaders.

He began his network marketing journey in 2009 while recovering from a career-halting injury as a full-time firefighter. Network marketing not only gave him a new path but also launched him into financial success in his thirties. He earned multiple accolades, including the highest award his company offered, and was honored with several magazine features and a cover story in *Success from Home*. Kirk reached a defining moment when he reached the top rank in the company while still balancing a full-time job as a firefighter.

In 2022, he transitioned to a new energy-focused network marketing company. The ground-floor opportunity reignited his drive, and he soon led one of the fastest-growing teams in the organization. He and his wife Trisha travel the country in their motor coach, building leaders and expanding their reach.

"I believe deeply in servant leadership," Kirk says. "When you genuinely care about people and invest in their growth, amazing things happen. I leverage a lifetime of diverse work experiences to connect with individuals from all walks of life, helping them see their potential and build their own successful businesses."

When not traveling for business or pleasure, Kirk and Trisha spend their time in Florida and the Northeast. They have two grown sons, Justin and Adam.

Website: ThinkEnergy.plus\HoranNrg

Facebook: Kirk M. Horan

Instagram: @KirkHoran

LinkedIn: Kirk Horan

It's All About Your Character, Not Your Past

JOHNNY WIMBREY, PH.D.

My childhood story is not a well-kept secret; in fact, I'm proud of it. When I was younger, I wrote a best-selling book, *From the Hood to Doing Good*, about how my experiences and choices, both good and bad, shaped me into who I am today and set me up for success. I often talk about the highs and lows I experienced growing up. My past is a part of my life, but it doesn't define me.

No, I wasn't a trust-fund baby, and there was never a silver spoon in my mouth. I didn't expect to inherit wealth or treasures because nobody in my family on either side—black or white—had much of anything. A trust fund was not something I'd ever imagined; growing up, I had no idea what it was. The concepts of an empire mindset or strategic wealth management were beyond me.

My earliest memories are of living in a shelter for battered women. I was a poor biracial kid from a broken home. My parents didn't have money, education, or significant jobs. I failed second grade, was arrested as a teenager, flirted with gang life, and nobody had any great expectations for me, if they even bothered to think about it.

But my life was never hopeless! My future was not preordained. Yes, my dad collected garbage and trash, but he worked incredibly hard, and I saw and learned to appreciate the effort he made every day. He realized there was more to life than the neighborhood we lived in, and he inspired my vision and hunger for a better life when he brought my wide-eyed brothers and me to see the mansions on his garbage truck route. Vision is created and enhanced by exposure, and I like to think my dad realized precisely what he was doing when he took us boys out in neighborhoods we'd never dreamed of until then. My dad gave us something to strive for. I was lucky to have him in my life for so many years.

My wife, Crystal, shares the responsibility for triggering the change in me from a teen who didn't think about the future to one who focused on making the right decisions about my faith and my life. I fell in love with Crystal when I was very young, and she saw something worthwhile in me that wasn't visible to most people. She and her parents had high expectations for me and my behavior, and they somehow knew I could meet them.

I did. Over the years, I have lived up to their expectations and established many of my own. Doing so was possible because my parents had laid the groundwork for the good character already inside me. Watching my dad do his job with dignity every day gave me an appreciation for his better character traits: determination, integrity, and loyalty.

For the first time, I began thinking about my future, rather than my past or present. Before I was 20, I decided and told myself *my past has no say in my future*. That decision shaped my mindset, ultimately affecting thousands of people I've worked with. It also led me to write my first bestseller while I was still in my twenties.

The following paragraph comes from Lao-Tzu, one of the more famous ancient Chinese philosophers, and not someone I usually quote. He wrote this about 26 centuries ago, and it still resonates:

Watch your thoughts, they become your words.
Watch your words, they become your actions.

Watch your actions, they become your habits.

Watch your habits, they become your character.

Watch your character; it becomes your destiny.

Once I had a glimpse of my potential destiny, I began to get the first glimmer of the depth and richness of what it means to have an empire mindset and create serious seven- or eight-figure generational wealth.

Let's not beat about the bush. I am talking about becoming a genuine, bona fide multimillionaire.

As I said, I started from scratch. My family had no way of giving me a boost. One generation of wealth can still make a difference for the next generation in this country, and I appreciate it from both sides of the financial divide. I've made sure trust funds are a solid foundation for the future of my three children, which is just a tiny part of what is meant by "generational wealth," as I learned in my twenties and continued to redefine in my thirties and forties. As I increase my wealth and reach my goals, I constantly redefine my definition of success and set new, more ambitious goals, and they're not all financial.

Do you refine your goals yearly?

If you don't, you should—and start now, because it's never too late.

Are you the same person at age 35 as you were at age 20, with the same goals? Is that even imaginable? Would you *want* to be mentally, financially, or emotionally in the same place?

Let's momentarily step back from the money; forget the outward trappings of success for now. The journey begins not with income but with introspection and building your foundation.

There is so much unseen work that goes into building the success I imagined—*and earned!*—for Crystal, our children, and myself. We all know that every building starts with a foundation. We accept that premise for physical buildings, but somehow, many people forget the same need regarding people and their accomplishments.

You don't build wealth from the outside in; you make it from the inside out. I hope you've heard this repeatedly, but it's worth repeating: *True success begins on the inside.*

Before you can even start thinking about money, you must—*must*—have a conversation with yourself about your character. Becoming a success, much less a multi-million-dollar success, has everything to do with the *character* you bring to the table. I'm talking about your true character, the person you are when nobody is around to see how you think and behave, or when rules are thrown out the window.

Success without character is fragile. It's fleeting. And when the applause fades, so does the identity. Money doesn't define you. It can't. You need to define the meaning of money as it applies to you, just as you define your comfort level with wealth.

If you want to change the trajectory of your life, change begins when you ask yourself one question: What kind of person am I when I'm alone and nobody is watching?

You need to know yourself and what you're capable of, without fooling yourself or putting on a front. You can never truly reach or maintain the definition of success without possessing untainted self-knowledge and a stable, optimistic character. With this honest knowledge and character, you learn to recognize yourself and encourage yourself to achieve success. When you achieve success as I define it, you have the basic building blocks for what I've written about in my most recent bestselling book, *Building a Millionaire Mindset.*

Every person I've mentored or coached to reach multi-million-dollar-producing status has something powerful within them—good, positive character and the ability to work hard. Each can also leave their past behind and look to the future. Their mindset is ripe for success.

I firmly believe that anyone who continuously works to develop their *internal* success or personal character can't help but also build *external* achievements. What all of us in On the Shoulders of Giants also have in common is that we're strategically creating, maintaining, and sustaining not just wealth but generational wealth.

When times are chaotic and the future is uncertain, it's even more vital to have inner strength and a positive outlook. Nothing stays the same in industry—who remembers the last "must-have" new product that failed miserably? Nothing stays the same in the world order, either. New alliances and enemies emerge year after year, or even month by month. Entire industries can vanish in weeks, but your character and mindset remain with you for your entire life. What you build with them can easily be sustainable for generations.

> " Success without character is fragile. "

You're ready to commit if you've read this far in my chapter and still agree with me.

Take a deep breath; your life will never be the same.

I invite you to join me and my dozen co-authors in the most exclusive group you could ever join: self-made multimillion- or billion-dollar producers of good character. We are all members, and we all built our success ourselves.

Before we proceed, please answer three questions.

- Do you value yourself? We're not talking about money but self-worth. If you genuinely want to succeed, you first need to understand and appreciate your abilities and their value. Unless you enjoy what you have and what you bring to conversations and meetings with others, you'll never have confidence in any situation. A lack of confidence will cause you to impose limits on yourself and, by extension, on what you bring to any business dealings.

- Do you have faith in yourself? If things get tough, if your product is replaced by a newer one in the marketplace, or if your secret sauce becomes everyday knowledge, do you believe you can remain creative and successful again? You can never have long-term success as a one-shot wonder.

- Do you have the commitment to give yourself—all of yourself—to your goals and projects? It takes your grit and perseverance. If you can't commit, you will stay mired just where you are.

Your character and mindset are built on a solid foundation; your values, faith, and commitment form the base of that foundation. No matter what knowledge, tools, and skills you add as you mature and grow, your success will inevitably fail without a strong foundation.

Let's talk more about these three invaluable and underlying characteristics of your character.

Value. Ever since I entered my twenties, I've been asked to speak with "at-risk" young people, an experience I enjoy and try to make enjoyable by sharing something they don't already know. One of my favorite talks is about their value as young individuals.

The first time I gave the talk, I had a great group of kids primed to learn the message. I got their attention when I reached into my pocket and pulled out a $100 bill. It was a new, crisp bill with Benjamin Franklin looking right at us all. After I showed it to the group, I asked, "How much is this worth?"

They took my softball question and didn't laugh as they sang out, "One hundred dollars." Then I folded it in half and asked them again, "How much is this worth?" They all agreed it was still worth $100. "Why? Why is it worth the same?" I asked, as innocently as I could.

"It doesn't matter if it's half the size; it's still the same. It's worth the same amount," the bravest ones answered.

I folded it into quarters. "It's tiny, just a little bit of the original bill. What's it worth now?" I asked. The children didn't waver. One hundred dollars.

I asked, "Even if it's just one-fourth of the original size, is it still worth the same?"

The kids had good manners, so they didn't laugh, "Of course!"

"What if I stomp on it, rub dirt on it, rip out a small chunk, and roll it up into a ball?"

"It's still worth $100," all the kids agreed, getting louder and more confident.

"No matter what, as long as it's mostly there, I can't do anything to make it worth less than its original value?" I asked.

They agreed.

"What happens to your value if someone stomps on you, damages you, and crumples you, emotionally or mentally? Will you lose your value?" I asked.

For once, they were quiet.

Then I asked, "How can a piece of fabric, a man-made object, retain its value more than you: a special, unique being, one in the image of the Creator?"

I could see lights go on in their eyes.

It may seem simplistic, but the concept can be hard to grasp: You must learn to value yourself to become truly successful. That was the conversation I needed when I was young.

And this is the conversation I'm having with you now.

You've been folded. You've been crumpled. You've been stepped on, but you still have your entire worth. Your value is non-negotiable. *If you don't believe in your value, no one else will.*

Value is evident in your posture, voice, and the way you enter a room. When you know who you are, people will treat you accordingly. But if you second-guess your place at the table, they'll assume you don't belong.

You were never designed to fit in.

You were created to stand out.

Let your value speak louder than your circumstances.

To accomplish anything substantial for the first time in your family, much less become a first-generation millionaire, means you've reached the understanding and the acceptance of personal value. You'll be stomped on during your journey to success, probably often, but you'll know nobody can take away your value.

Faith. When I refer to faith, I'm not talking about religious faith but about your faith in *yourself*. I'll have questions for you to answer, but first, let's consider what you don't hesitate to have faith in, despite its complexity and unreliability. Think about the last time you drove your car. You went out, unlocked it, climbed in the driver's seat, fastened the seatbelt, started the engine, and selected the right gear. You didn't kick each tire and check its pressure; you didn't do the equivalent of a pre-flight checklist before turning over the engine, and no co-pilot told you the brake light worked.

You don't ask to see the driver's safety and car maintenance records when you climb into an Uber. You have faith that unless something triggers your sixth sense, you will be fine in a situation you chose with your eyes wide open.

Do you have at least that much faith in yourself? Do you continue on your path once a situation has begun, or do you doubt yourself in a flood of double-guessing? Many people have a steady backbeat of doubts: *They'll think I'm an idiot. They'll say NO. I'll never get the deal to go through. I'm going home.*

Do you realize your car will likely break down more than you will? Unfortunately, you're more likely to trust your vehicle than your own decisions, even when you know you skipped the recommended maintenance for your old vehicle.

Why? Why do you have more faith in the driver's well-used Uber and his *5-Hour Energy* drink than you do in your ability to become a millionaire? You *must* have faith in yourself, or you will never succeed. Faith doesn't mean you won't have fear. Of course you will.

If fear rules us, we hesitate. We second-guess. We don't launch the business, make the call, or take the leap. Why? Because deep down, we don't trust that we're enough.

Let me say this: **You are more than enough.**

When you think about yourself, what do you believe in? What about your talents? Your work ethic? Do you have faith in your ability to communicate and in your ability to make good decisions?

My faith in myself continues to prove itself, and it's only grown stronger over the last three decades. I consciously nurture it. I know we must maintain faith in ourselves and our abilities. When we don't, the very first wave will wash us away, not even leaving our footprints. When we maintain personal faith in ourselves, we tap into much higher levels of personal success.

> " You must learn to value yourself, or you will never become truly successful. "

My faith has rewarded me very well. Every time I take a big step forward, I take a risk. I can take the risk because I have faith in myself. If I'd failed, I could have gone underwater financially. Instead, I leapfrogged ahead. If I hadn't had that faith, I'd still live in the same house I built when Crystal and I married 27 years ago. Even building that modest two-story house was a leap of faith. Of course, every big decision since then has also been a leap of faith, and each one is easier.

I haven't taken the easy path. I haven't needed to. I had faith in myself. *That's the type of faith you need, the bedrock of your success.* Faith isn't hoping the door opens someday. Faith is building the door, carving the doorknob, and kicking it open when it is right.

Commitment. Commitment is what separates the dabblers from the doers. It isn't sexy. It's not usually exciting. It's working early mornings. It's staying up late to get the job done. It's doing the things no one sees, so that everyone sees what you've done one day. Commitment means making the uncomfortable non-negotiable.

Commitment must be your definition of the term, not someone else's. Working under someone else's vision is perfectly acceptable when you're beginning your journey. I did. I served. I followed. I learned. But I didn't stay there. I didn't make someone else's dream permanent while neglecting my own.

Your definition, however, should include "personal connection" in its terminology. That's its common denominator. If you can't relate personally to your project or connect in some way to its end goal, be forewarned: This is not your project, no matter how much you may have thought it was.

That said, it's hard to have your own worthwhile projects when you are starting out. Working on someone else's commitment will expose you to new ideas, improve your skills, and help you learn what your projects might be. You can find your value in raising their work. Work with someone else when you begin so you'll learn to define what you love. You can still use your style and put your mark on the project. Use these experiences as a jumping-off point before committing to your unique project.

I have no doubt you'll find your project when the time is right. You know intuitively what you're excellent at doing. We *all* excel at something. It's too easy to hide behind someone else's definition of greatness and choose their project, so don't get too comfortable. You'll find yourself trying to convince your inner self it's safer and a lot less risky to stay where you are, being more secure, working on that other person's project. Think about it—you know better. Just because someone says you're the best salesperson, promoter, or marketing mind on their project, it doesn't mean you can't be better and do better on your own projects.

Once you commit, commit fully. Don't start negotiating with yourself and rationalize why you no longer need to take the next step. You're not committed if you find yourself making excuses for no longer needing to get up early to research leads or work late to make calls. You're just going through the motions. *STOP! You can't* negotiate commitment. You can negotiate many aspects of how you live and interact, but you cannot negotiate your commitment to the journey. You need to commit 100 percent to this lifelong adventure.

Let's take this a step further. Stop if you know you're not able to give your all to any of these three: value, faith, *or* commitment. Wait until you're ready to be serious about doing whatever it takes to become a millionaire. Wait until it's no longer an option, but a necessity. Wait until you're ready to become a giant yourself.

Character. Value, faith, and commitment are the foundation of your *character*, the building blocks of your life, leading to true success. Your character allows you to keep and enjoy your success throughout your lifetime.

Your character is more important than any traditional marker of success. Your character will keep you going when you've had a failure. Your character will be passed on to your children and their children, preserving true generational wealth within your family. No matter how many classes or programs you take, how many speeches you sit through, or how many mentors you work with, none of them will help or mean a thing unless you've also worked on your character.

If you are to be a millionaire of good character who doesn't lose what you've done, you need to have faith in yourself. You must value what you bring to the table. And you must commit to your cause. If you have little faith, don't understand your value, and argue with yourself about what you promised to do, you won't make it. Don't be embarrassed because most people can't; they're not yet ready to change their lives. They're not prepared to do the work.

Success is standing right in front of you. Build and maintain your true character—who you are when it is just you and yourself. Laying that foundation is the first step to becoming a first-generation millionaire.

The many times my dad took me to see those mansions on his garbage route exposed me to a future I could begin to envision— something bolder. Dad might not have known the mechanics of legacy-building, but he laid the foundation with his character—every early morning, I saw him go to work, and every route he drove was through generational wealth, even if it wasn't his own.

That's the kind of father he was. That's the kind of man I chose to become. My conscious choices were very different, with proportionately larger outcomes, but the foundation was laid when I was young.

I'm not just a product of exposure. I'm a result of evolution. And this is what I want you to know right out of the gate: *Becoming a first-generation multi-million-dollar-producer is not about making money, it's about forging character.*

While you must look forward to the future, keep the faith, and not live in the past, you can't leave it all behind as much as you'd like to forget your less memorable actions. When you engage in thoughtless, angry, or uncontrolled actions, they can significantly impact your reputation and future, and may be impossible to shake, especially in the era of widespread social media. You are the sum of your actions and your mistakes—as I learned when I was still a teenager, thankfully. I didn't have to drag much of my bad baggage to adulthood; what came with me was fixable. In my case, I didn't have much to lose when I made the quantum shift in my life to a new, positive behavior and mindset. Thirty years ago, memories were much shorter than they are now.

The smartphone has made you more vulnerable than ever to self-imposed damage. Now, any ten-year-old can make a video of you misbehaving in a full-blown moment of anger or stupidity, and it will live forever on the world's stage. We often see people at the top levels dodge silver bullets, but most of us don't have access to a top-notch team of publicists. The dings and bumps to our reputations will live forever in our virtual friends' and enemies' memories and news feeds. Lose your temper in the wrong way and the wrong place, and you may never live it down.

I've phrased the approach I use and recommend to my followers as "becoming a friend to your future self." I don't mean an enabler or instigator. I'm referring to the kind of friend who truly cares about you, your well-being, and your life.

Once you're looking ahead to your new future and can consistently visualize it, you also want to start protecting that future self. Taking responsibility and learning to control your temper and actions is a matter of taking responsibility. You need to learn to respond rather than react to situations. You can learn this—I did!

> " I'm here to remind you: If I can do it, so can you. "

One of the most challenging things I've done is learn to control my temper. Mine is sizzling hot, and it often has a mind of its own. When I was starting a family and a business, I realized that I couldn't risk losing it all over an argument or an idiot with a bad attitude. I'd left guns behind years ago, but my path was still strewn with traps that could swallow my future.

As I developed self-control and refined my diplomatic skills, I became stronger, better, and more capable of achieving my goals. I'd been taught never to back down, to give as good as I got, and I needed to unlearn that mindset, become more peaceable, and develop a longer fuse. I can resist more temptations than I would have dreamed when I was a hot-blooded 17-year-old.

It's still hard, surprisingly so. If you walked up and punched me, I don't know if I could defuse the situation, much less turn the other cheek. I'd definitely do my damn best. The thought of seeing myself on the evening news, not winning an award or giving a speech, but brawling with some idiot or doing the perp walk with a coat over my head, keeps my worst tendencies in check. My better self is sitting on my shoulder, offering reinforcement, whispering into my ear, telling me to calm down and be the best kind of friend rather than yelling bloodthirsty encouragements that would escalate the situation.

As I aged, I discovered new potential dangers to my future successful self. My family has a history of heart disease that takes down the Wimbrey men before their time. I thought I was healthy and fit until I had to pay a higher premium on my new life insurance policy because of a high cholesterol test result. My doctor gave me options, and I took the hard way—better diet and more exercise. I knew it was time for change and managed to reverse what was happening to me.

Now, at 50, I'm healthier and fitter than I was at 20. I can clearly see the many dimensions of my goals, and I want to enjoy their full richness with my wife, three kids, and future generations of my family.

Think about it: Do you want to be a financially successful leader who's mastered growth and scale, fabulously wealthy but with bad lungs and heart, and unable to make the most of your enviable life? *Invest in yourself now.*

Don't forget what's above your neck! Invest in self-improvement courses, videos, seminars, and meetings. Over the last thirty years, I've spent hundreds of thousands of dollars getting exceptional input, training, advice, and time with the best of the best. I wouldn't be who I am or where I am now without the invaluable help of my mentors, the people who became my modern-day giants, the ones who gave me a boost so I could see further.

I'm not here to impress you. I'm here to remind you: *If I can do it, so can you.*

I went from a shelter to a stage, from poverty to power. My most outstanding achievement is that my children will never experience the chaos from which I came. They'll know the story but not the struggle. I want them to inherit spiritual, emotional, and mental wealth, reinforced by their good character. They're standing on my shoulders, and yes, they *can* see further.

Now it's your turn. Stand on my shoulders. Look ahead.

Then become the giant you were born to be!

ABOUT JOHNNY WIMBREY

Johnny Wimbrey has one of the most intriguing and successful rags-to-riches stories of this century, rising from a teenage felon to become a multi-million-dollar producer, a world-renowned speaker, author, motivator, and coach.

His many best-selling books include **Building a Millionaire Mindset**, a serious guide to successful entrepreneurship offered by the premier educational publisher in the United States, and **From the Hood to Doing Good,** a memoir written while he was in his twenties.

Johnny's wholly owned Mpower Empire's international clients include world-famous athletes, politicians, and elite leaders. A separate division, Wimbrey Training Systems, publishes most of his books and many of his co-authors' titles. Top WTS bestsellers include **Multiple Streams of Inspiration** and **The Power of Mental Wealth**, and the company is publishing the guaranteed bestselling *Stand on the Shoulders of Giants* series.

Johnny has worked and done projects with most of the top names in personal development, including the legendary grandfathers of the field, Les Brown, Zig Ziglar, and Jim Rohn. During his appearances around the globe, he has mentored and coached hundreds of thousands of elite leaders and multi-million-dollar producers.

Johnny's childhood was fraught; he grew up as a biracial child from a broken family in one of the most dangerous and gang-ridden neighborhoods in Texas. His first memory was of a homeless shelter. As a teen headed for trouble, he was charged with a felony. His life turned around when he fell in love and focused instead on his character and future.

He and his wife, Crystal, along with their daughters, Hannah and Psalms, and son, Honor, live in North Central Texas.

 Wimbrey.com

 Facebook: JohnnyWimbrey

 Instagram: @wimbrey

Do Something Great

CAL QUIGLEY IV, PH.D.

No matter what else I do, it's important for me to always find time to mentor or inspire others who grew up in places like Johnny Wimbrey and I did—the Stop Six neighborhood in southeast Fort Worth, a high-crime, high-unemployment minority community as infamous as Watts or the South Side of Chicago.

Back in the late '70s, and early '80s, Stop Six wasn't a lethal place to live. We could ride bicycles and play football in the street. People thought, *"This is the quintessential Black community, and it's going to raise some of the best leaders of this generation."* But by the late '80s, drugs had moved across our country, Fort Worth became a distribution hub, and the neighborhood became a war zone overnight.

Many of the survival skills I learned in my neighborhood translated well into my military career. I served in Operation Enduring Freedom, and I always slept like a baby through bombs and shooting. My years in the Fort Worth war zone and hearing gunshots all night had numbed me. In the back of my mind, I knew which caliber they were shooting and how far away they were, and I could ignore the craziness.

Unlike my friends, I was lucky to spend most of my childhood in a two-parent household. My parents were married very young, and my dad, Cal, joined the Air Force and then worked for Lockheed Martin. My mom, Marcia, was a nurse. For the most part, I had a stable middle-class home. Outside the doors, it was a different environment. When the gangs started to infiltrate the neighborhood, I saw many of my friends getting caught up and becoming gangbangers themselves, pushing dope or becoming shooters for those gangs. Of the 20 friends I grew up with, all but two of us have served time in a federal prison. I'm not saying I never did anything stupid. I still cringe when I think of the "Fight Club" we had in the summers when our parents were at work. My saving grace was playing sports. Ironically, the first time I saw someone get shot, I was about 13 and walking home from practice. A guy was walking down the street in a pair of new Jordans when a car pulled up, and a guy said, "Hey, kick your shoes off! We'll take those!" The kid didn't want to give up his shoes; when he tried to run away, they shot him twice in the back and pulled off his shoes.

At home, I had no therapy and no talking about what had happened. My parents said, "Get your homework done, and tomorrow we'll pray you make it home safely. Take another route to make sure you don't run into the same guys." There was no empathy for the child who died.

The first time I went to a gang party, I didn't know what I was walking into. It was a 16th birthday party filled with people I knew. Everybody there was banging except for me and one friend. That day a 9-mm pistol was put in my face for the first time (but not the last).

That was when fathers started disappearing. The father of one of my good friends had been in the Navy, and he was a tall, handsome, well-dressed man. When he started doing crack, he quickly devolved into a bum, always trying to get a couple of dollars from you, essentially turning into a pariah. That affected not just my friend, but his sisters as well.

My house was a safe haven for my friends with some semblance of peace, and they'd come over and hang out. I had a basketball hoop in the backyard and we would always play until the lights came on. I was so thankful my father never got caught up in drugs like so many dads. He was a drinker, and he'd have episodes where he might turn up drunk occasionally, but the next morning he would get up, make everybody breakfast, clean up the house, and go to work. Until I was about 15, he helped me navigate my options and kept me out of a lot of trouble, but then my parents got divorced, and he was on the other side of town with his new family. At least I had those first 15 years with my father present to offer guidance.

The first 6½ years of my life gave me a solid foundation and a big edge in experience and confidence. My dad was part of General Dynamics (Lockheed Martin's) developmental plan team. When he traveled to Egypt, Venezuela, Greece, Israel, and Pakistan, the entire family joined him. I started school in Cairo, Egypt, and Arabic was one of my first languages. I spent my early formative years among people who were not the same as me. The practical education I received from my travels and the exotic experiences enriched my life forever. When things were rough, I could always go back in my memory to a place I chose, let's say the Acropolis, and I'm sitting there looking at 14,000 years of history.

The other key advantage I had was an innate love of learning, which my mother encouraged. I'd come home, have a snack, relax for a few minutes, and get right into the books. I was an avid reader, and very early on, I was taught how to research. I can still see the encyclopedias in the bookcase in the hall. The *Encyclopedia Britannica* was the first internet as far as Momma was concerned. Whenever I had a question about something, she never said, "Oh, I don't know." Instead, she said, "Go grab that encyclopedia, figure it out, and then come back and tell me the answer to the question." I was taught very early on to be able to fend for myself and research.

Momma often told me I was special, repeating a story of when we were in Egypt and a man walked up to us on the street and announced,

"There's one of our kings" as he pointed to me. As I grew up, she'd remind me, "You're a king. You're different, and you're supposed to do something great." My friends didn't get much of that instilled in them; instead, they received a lot of negative messages at home.

From an early age, I tried to share the love and encouragement that I was getting at home and bring it to my friends at school. It helped that I played all the sports—baseball, football, basketball, golf—and I always was the positive guy on the team. You'd hear me being loud and happy: "Come on, we can do it, even though we're down 30, you know we can do it!"

I was 17 years old when I enlisted in the Air Force and 18 when I arrived at my first post. I remember it like it was yesterday: It was December 6, 1996. The temperature was 85°F when I boarded the plane in Texas. When I stepped out of the plane in North Dakota, the temperature was -5°F, and the wind was blowing. I stopped dead and said aloud, "Oh, hell naw! This ain't gonna work. Get me outta here." There was no sun for six months, it was snowing and windy every day, and it was an experience different than anything I had ever imagined.

Soon I realized I was depressed. I wasn't alone. Grand Forks Air Force Base had the highest suicide rate in the military for service members under 21. I knew I had to figure something out, so I signed up for college classes for the spring semester. I'm not proud of how I handled my transportation challenge, because I stole a kid's bike from the base and rode to my night classes. I justified it as pure survival tactics. I was still rationalizing a few things I shouldn't, but I was working on that.

I didn't know what I wanted to do, had no real goals, and didn't meet with an academic advisor. I just knew I needed to be *learning*. The wheels in my head needed to spin, or I was going to do something bad to myself.

Education was my reprieve; it was my therapy. I realized very quickly that learning was going to be a lifelong journey for me, not just something I was trying in order to check a box off in the military. Education is still a life-enriching hobby for me (along with golf). But I couldn't play golf in North Dakota in the winter and keep myself busy and positive. Statistics showed what happened to people who came from the South and ended up in these places. The odds were I was going to start drinking, live a borderline illegal life, and get into trouble. I was attempting my own rescue. I had my classes, but I needed more.

There are three core values of the Air Force: *Integrity first, service before self,* and *excellence in all we do.* I decided to adopt them and apply them to my actions and life.

Regarding *integrity*, I vowed never to steal again, no matter how I could rationalize it. And I haven't. I've broadened my definition of the term since then, but honesty was a good start.

> " There are three core values of the Air Force: *Integrity first, service before self, and excellence in all we do.* I decided to adopt them and apply them to my actions and life. "

When it came to *excellence*, my depressed 18-year-old mind recalled what my mother told me all those years about the Egyptian man saying I was a king, going to become great, and with a bigger calling. I realized the excellence that was in me hadn't shown itself yet, and I had to allow myself to mature and get to the point where it would.

Service before self seemed simple. I've always prided myself on never being a hater, always trying to motivate people and helping them to get to the next level. That was a good start, but I knew there was so much more I could learn. I wondered how I could surround myself with people who are better at learning so I could then share what I'm good at with them as well.

But I needed mentors. I found some amazing ones in the military, some people who saw in me what I couldn't yet see in myself. My first one was not at all what I expected.

There in cold, dark North Dakota, my job was hospital administration. I hated it. This just added to the desperation of trying to figure out how to get out of the unhappy situation I was in. My first desperately needed mentor showed up, Master Sergeant Marge Wisniewska, a Caucasian lady from Wisconsin. She came in to see me one day and asked quietly, "Why do you always look so down?"

I didn't hesitate. "Well, I hate it here, and I hate what I do. And this wasn't what I expected being in the military to be about." This was 1996, between the Gulf wars, and there wasn't a lot going on in peacetime.

She asked, "What would you do if I could wave a magic wand?"

I pointed to the computer room filled with Airmen with swag and said, "I want to be one of those guys." The computer room is where the elite in our squadron were kept; they used to call them the "computer gods" back then.

I was on a roll, trying to be very positive. "I would rather be doing what those guys do because they're sharp. They look like they're having a real impact on the actual mission. They're making things happen while I'm pushing paperwork. This isn't what I want to do."

Within 60 days, I was out of medical records, and I was in there with the computer gods. That changed the entire trajectory of my life, of my career, of everything. My new position finally gave me direction in college, and I started taking computer science classes.

That wasn't the first or last time I talked with Sergeant Wisniewska. We had good conversations, where she asked me about my background and why I joined the Air Force. I told her of my goals, that I was going to college, and why I wanted to escape the gang-ridden place where I'd be dead in four to five years if I'd stayed.

Even before my life-changing moment, I was aware I was being observed. There weren't many Black men on that base, so I didn't want to be lumped in with everyone else. I kept my uniforms squared away, my hair edged as sharply as I could do it by myself, extra neat and presentable. And I was always professional—even when I was depressed and hated what I was doing. If someone came in and needed something, I was Johnny-on-the-spot: *What can I do to help you?*

I tried to be a stand-up guy. They were paying me. They gave me an opportunity. I'd signed up for the college money. I accepted and respected what happened and always tried to be as positive as I could in what was a really bad situation for me.

In 1999, in Korea, Master Sergeant Jones took me under his wing and helped me get into the real estate game. He was a short little Black guy from Chicago, but the real deal, all the way around. He knew my next duty station was going to be in the District of Columbia, and he explained what to look for in investing and whether to buy a condominium or a house to start building generational wealth. That was the first time anybody had ever shared information like that. Just as important, he was also teaching me how to navigate and succeed in the military as a Black man.

With his guidance, I tested for and was promoted to staff sergeant when I was 22 years old which was extremely young. Being a staff sergeant meant whenever I barked, "We're gonna run into this building and blow it up," thirty people were right there following my lead. Master Sergeant Jones helped me navigate my new-found rank. He explained, "You're about to be in charge of people in their thirties and forties. You can't be the 22-year-old hotshot E5 that you are. It won't work out very well. They will eat you alive." I loved that guy, and I will always appreciate what he did for me.

Sergeant Jones taught me people are always watching you. If you're the man in the arena you know all eyes are on you as soon as you walk in the building; sometimes even when you're still in the parking lot. I've had people tell me they watched me walk from my car to the building and judged me by the speed and purpose of my walk.

When I talk to someone who's got eyes on them, I say, "Yes, everybody's watching. Assume they're watching every move that you make to see if you have confidence at all times."

As you're making decisions as the leader in the group, you need to think about the decisions through the lens of your leadership, not just what's going to be best for you. Through Master Sergeant Jones and even earlier, through my parents and sports, I learned that bringing everyone to the table and making a collective decision is best. No one wants to be dictated to, even if you're in a position to do so.

When I look back on the first 45 years of my life, I submit I have tried to live with no regrets. I try to accept the results of my actions, good or bad. I do have one major regret, though. When my son was born, I was 22 years old and in an uncommitted relationship. Unfortunately, that happens too often to young people in the military. I wasn't prepared for the responsibility of fatherhood and was an absentee dad. If I could go back and do that all over again, I would do it differently.

If I could talk to my 22-year-old self, I would say, "Cal, you've got to get some counseling. You have so much baggage from the situation with your father you haven't gotten past, even though you're pretending it never bothered you." I didn't fight for visitation rights as hard as I could have; I let the courts dictate the level of my parenting because of my feelings of defeat.

Yes, that's definitely a regret. If I could talk to him now or in the future, I would say, "I love you, man, I love you. I always did. Part of the reason why I didn't fight as hard as I could is because I felt like it would damage you more. But again, I could have done a better job of being there for you."

Since I've started teaching at Texas Christian University, I tell my students a story on the first day of each semester. The story has two purposes: It adds credibility to who I am, and it also shows my transparency as a professor.

When I was finishing my undergraduate degree in 2004-2005, I had to come up with a business plan for a senior project. The United States was at war, and I realized the Air Force had changed the way we could get food delivered on base. Imagine this: You're a young soldier chilling in your room. You've been working all day, and you want to have a couple of beers before ordering food. Before the war, you'd stay in your room, call, and get food from any off-base restaurant. They'd come on base, knock on your door, and deliver the food. No problem.

Then we had Al-Qaeda and security was tight—no delivery people were allowed on base. Now the young beer-drinking soldiers needed to get into their cars and drive very, very carefully to the front gate to meet the delivery drivers. If they swerved just a little bit and the lights from the military police hit them, their careers could be over, thanks to a DUI.

> " What can I do to give back to my community? "

My concept was to set up a delivery service owned and run by members of the military. Background checks would already be in place so they could come on and go off base. No problem, no breach in security, no DUIs.

I wrote the paper, scored well, and my professor said, "This is an excellent plan. Did you ever think about making it into a real business? I think it could be lucrative."

No, I hadn't. I was just trying to get an A and get out of his class so I could graduate. He kept badgering me. I was in DC at the time, and I called my cousin, Heronn Harrison, who was there, too; he'd just finished his master's degree in marketing. I said, "I wrote this paper; my professor thinks it's really good. You're somebody I trust. What do you think?"

Heronn got back to me in two days. He had put an entire detailed business plan together, even designed logos, and he said, "This is it. You need to sell everything you own, put the cash into this, and we're going to do it." He was serious. The name of the company was Cousin's Delivery.

We convinced restaurants to turn to-go orders into delivery orders. When you called Pappadeaux Seafood Kitchen and said, "I want to order the Pasta Mardi Gras," the restaurant asked, "Would you like to have it delivered to your quarters on base for an additional $5?" If you said yes, the restaurant called our company and gave us the order. We picked it up, paid for it with our credit card, got a discount as our contract was structured, and we charged you full price.

We made a 16 percent profit, not counting the delivery fee or tip, for a total of about $15-18 per delivery. We ran the company for two years in Arlington before UberEats was a glimmer in Uber's eye. Fast forward to 2008, the housing crisis was beginning, there was an economic meltdown, the government was going into lockdown, restaurants were shutting down, and we closed. Temporarily, I thought.

A company reached out to me and asked to purchase my data, but I didn't understand what that meant back then. They called and called, and I was determined not to sell, stubbornly thinking *I created this, it's mine, and I'm going to open it up again someday.*

Our corporate suitor turned out to be Uber—and we missed the opportunity to do a major merger and acquisition deal. My cousin and I might be billionaires now.

How should I have handled it, with full benefit of hindsight?

Obviously, I would have sold them the data. But I'd also have set up a contract for me to serve on the Uber board in perpetuity. There are many intelligent choices I would know to make now. At the very least, I would have formed a partnership with them. Looking back, I would have taken on business debt and partners. I'd financed the entire business by selling my real estate portfolio, but now I have a much more nuanced understanding of debt than I did as an undergraduate.

I tell this story every semester at TCU's Neely School of Business where I teach, and I get the credibility that comes from telling the story because students do their research and look up Cousin's. They learn I'm telling the truth. The rest of the semester is solid gold. People were calling me a genius, there were articles in the paper, and I admit I enjoyed the kudos. I also enjoyed our first month in the black, when we made a $30,000 profit.

It was great to be validated. Even if it didn't turn out as well as it could have, that's a lesson learned. Whatever disappointment came from that missed opportunity has galvanized me into the next phase of my life.

We've talked about excellence, integrity, and service as my core values. When I start thinking about what will drive me to the next level, I know it's persistence and trust in my community. I wasn't the only one who made my first company work. I couldn't deliver, drive, and answer the phone, so I had to start relying on people and developing a community around me with the same goals and aspirations to see something grow from nothing.

My faith in God kept me centered through any disappointments. It kept me in line, and I could hear God say quietly, "You weren't ready."

This triggered a reset in my thinking. I did a complete 180 and switched from trying to be a titan of industry to asking, *"What can I do to give back to my community?"*

My wife Jessica's background is in financial services; we believe academic programs need restructuring to include financial literacy. We started going into the schools to teach not only financial literacy but business planning as well, and we brought a curriculum to fourth, seventh, and twelfth graders. We created Quantum Prosperus, a financial services company that includes the Legacy Wealth Academy, a year-long financial empowerment educational program for anyone from students to retirees. Jessica is the driving force behind our financial services company, my full partner as well as my wife.

Jessica and I have been together for 22 years and married for 17 and actions. I realize whenever I want something in this life, I don't hesitate—I go after it.

I'm grateful for being able to break the generational pattern I was born into: being trapped in jobs, owing money, punching a time clock, and having limited impact on others' lives. I live life on my own terms, yet I never take it for granted. I'm grateful for all the freedom I have.

Financial freedom means so much more than just money. Now I can spend my time doing what I love most—spending time with my wife and family and helping people make better lives. At the moment I write this, I am traveling through the Rocky Mountains, enjoying the luxury of financial freedom while my team continues to grow.

of them. She is a first-generation American with Mexican roots, the oldest of six children. Her parents never made it past sixth grade, and they've worked hard in the agriculture industry their entire lives—seven days a week, 24 hours a day. She's always said she wanted to take care of her parents, and I supported her wholly in that. Two years ago, we were able to build a home in Mexico and allow her parents to retire. That action removed so much pressure from Jessica; I felt proud of myself for being able to help our family.

Growing up, I always thought money was the thing that made someone successful. I was sure true success was making a million dollars. When I made my first million, I kept waiting for balloons and music. None of that happened, and I thought, *Okay, I guess I need to get back to work.*

Now I'm 46 going on 47 and I still have a lot to learn about success as well as life. But being able to see the people I've impacted and how I've helped them get to the next level is more important than just money in our hands. We have created seven six-figure earners in our organization. They're helping other people on their team or in their family, helping them build the same kind of success we've seen. That's satisfying to me. I'm on a variety of boards of trustees, and I work with nonprofits and for-profits, giving back to them as well.

Every year, Jessica and I take the last day of the year, check into a hotel, and we totally unplug. We use this uninterrupted time to create our dream board for the upcoming year, focusing on five things: faith, family, finance, fitness, and fun.

For years we wanted to finance a dedicated building for our church, and a few years ago, we were in the position to buy a shopping center. We bought out everybody's leases, gutted it, all 30,000 square feet of it, and today it's our church. On one side, we have a sanctuary, and on the other, an event center where we host weddings and conferences. In the middle are suites, one for my office, one for teenagers and children to hang out during Sunday and Wednesday services. When I think back, I smile. The church was on our dream board back in 2010, and we prayed, meditated, and made decisions as we worked toward that vision. Now 500 members enjoy a beautiful, functional physical space every week at Trinity Harvest Church.

Writing down your vision is *the* most important thing. Someone taught me very early in my adult life: *If you don't write it down, it doesn't exist.* I can entertain myself for hours with whatever is floating in my head, but until I get it on paper, it doesn't exist.

> " Progress cannot be made on intentions alone "

Once it's written, meditate on it. You also must share with your teammates so everybody knows their own role; this applies to how you communicate with your family as well. It's like being coach of a football team. If the wide receiver doesn't know he's to run a slant, then the quarterback may let a deep post fly instead. Make sure everybody knows their position, their route, and what they're a part of for your dream board to work.

In the room Jessica and I share, we put our dream board where most people hang their TV. It's the first thing we see every morning, and it's the last thing we see at night. We take what we put on the board very seriously; every day we're working toward something on that board.

It's not enough just to hope for something. Yes, God appreciates your positive attitude, but he's more appreciative when you put some work behind the hope. Put in some muscle, hard work, fortitude, and real commitment behind your hopes. God will take it from there.

I hope people know Cal Quigley IV loves God, his family, and his community, because those are the things that are most important to me. Everything I have is tied to God because he gave them to me: He gave me a beautiful wife, a beautiful son, and a beautiful daughter. Of course, I want to leave them in a good financial position, because Proverbs 13:22 tell us "A good person leaves an inheritance for their children's children." This inheritance is intangible as well, for I love them, I always think and care about them, and above all, I'm not perfect.

I hope my community is part of my legacy—what we do through our financial literacy outreach and our financial services company, and what I'm doing at Texas Christian University now, creating financial wealth for our student athletes by teaching them how to invest the money that's pouring in with the new revenue source they have via their names, images, and likeness (NILs) deals.

The first time I was called in to talk to these young athletes, it was pro bono. I like helping people, especially our young men of color, and I take it seriously. I don't do much for free anymore, but when I got a call that our young athletes were putting themselves in some questionable circumstances, burning holes in their pockets with the sudden influx of NIL money, and needing my help, I was there.

Now I'm working with the football, basketball, and soccer teams, helping them manage and grow their money. Through our financial services company, we're able to teach them and help them build generational wealth.

I came from an environment where college wasn't very important. When I was just 22, I thought my future would be to retire from the military, play golf, smoke cigars, and travel. Now I have five degrees in five different fields. As I tell my students, each of my degrees puts me in a position to be able to pivot; that's important because every five or six years, I am driven to do something totally different. It's just the way I'm built. When I finish a degree, I do that work for a few years as I start thinking about what my next plan will be.

Though I'd never planned to be a college professor, my dissertation fit right into my life. I wrote about young men of color and how using the GI Bill changes the future of their families. It certainly changed mine.

My next plan is already in the works. I've never grown trees or plants, or shown that I'm good with my hands, but that time is coming. I've learned progress cannot be made on intentions alone. It'll be time soon for me to try something absolutely new—all over again.

ABOUT CAL QUIGLEY IV, Ph.D.

Dr. Quigley is the Chief Investment Strategist and Founder of Quantum Prosperus, a Professor of Global Business, Investments, and Ethics at the Neeley School of Business at Texas Christian University (TCU), and a community philanthropist.

Cal and his wife Jessica launched Quantum Prosperus, an innovative financial literacy community with comprehensive resources and real-world strategies usually available only to the wealthy. The personalized support revolutionizes financial education for families and young individuals, offering insights into business, finance, investing, and entrepreneurship. Their mission is to empower individuals with practical strategies tailored to their goals, amplifying their potential to build generational wealth and financial freedom.

Expanding on this vision, they co-founded Legacy Wealth Academy, equipping people with the knowledge and tools to take control of their financial futures. The Academy provides a step-by-step approach to financial literacy—guiding members from budgeting fundamentals to investment strategies—ensuring they gain the confidence to build and sustain wealth on their own terms.

ABC recognized Cal for his podcast "Wallet and Wellness," bridging the gap between mental wellness and financial freedom. Through candid conversations with seasoned investors and financial experts, the show provides practical insights and real-life stories that help listeners navigate their own financial journeys.

Beyond his work with Quantum Prosperus, Cal is committed to mentoring and educating individuals—including business owners, professionals, and student-athletes—on financial literacy and wealth-building strategies. As part of his work, he advises athletes navigating NIL (Name, Image, and Likeness) deals, helping them make informed financial decisions that support long-term success.

Cal is deeply passionate about equipping people with the knowledge and tools to take control of their financial and professional futures, guiding them with mentorship, resources, and actionable strategies.

 QPWealthHub.com

 @calquig & @quantumprosperus

 @CalQuigleyIV

 @CalQuigleyIV & @quantumprosperus

You Go Farther When You're On a Team

CHRIS ROBINETTE

When I rejoined the civilian world after 11 years in the Navy, I had a brand-new divorce, a shiny new MBA, and many invitations to take the easy path to Wall Street and mint money. For years, Wall Street had been where I was sure I belonged. Instead, I looked inside myself and thought about what happened to my family five years before. I remembered my 19-year-old sister and my 23-year-old self dealing with my mother's estate, without a clue of what she intended. I decided to take a huge risk and change the trajectory of my life.

Without looking back, I moved to Nashville, a town I'd never lived in before, and began a financial planning and risk-management career. It was a complete turnaround from the Navy or doing big-time mergers and acquisitions, but I was determined to help families and children and protect the hard work that their parents had done. I didn't want anyone to go through what my sister and I had endured.

My mom passed away a year after I'd graduated from the Naval Academy, and I was headed to Iraq when word reached me. My ship was crossing the Andaman Sea off the coast of Thailand, entering the Indian

Ocean; we couldn't stop, turn around, and put me on a helicopter because we were mission-critical. I knew I needed to get back to Oklahoma to help take care of all that had to be done. It was just my teenage sister and my grandparents trying to do it all. Our stepfather was being unhelpful.

I tried to coordinate what needed to be done with my sister and my grandparents over an obscenely expensive satellite phone, but we could talk so little they were mostly on their own. I rode the ship seven more days before I could start to Oklahoma and help my family; it was ten days after my mom died before I finally got home. I had never even read the trust document at that point.

A lot of bad decisions were made and inexplicable things happened in my absence. My grandparents were with my mother when she passed away, but when they went home to Kentucky for 24 hours, important works of art disappeared, cash and bank statements vanished, and all of her paperwork was shredded for absolutely no logical reason. It couldn't be explained away like a sudden burst of irrational grief. When we asked, our stepdad just said, "Well, we didn't need those documents anymore."

My teenage sister had been tasked with doing everything related to the family trust because she was physically closer to the lawyers, papers, and brokers. While I was trying to coordinate with her and my grandparents from the ship, she had been convinced that we'd lose about $1.5 million if the estate went to probate, and instead, she should give that money to our stepdad to save taxes. This was dead wrong. The estate would not have gone to probate, but my sister believed what she was told. I didn't have the knowledge at the time to help her follow my mother's wishes and resist misinformation.

It wasn't as though my mother had mishandled her estate planning; she just kept all her plans quiet and private. Her estate was first-generation wealth, all her own earnings and investments, and she intended for it to go to my sister and me and our future families. She had no experience in how to prepare us or share her wishes, and she'd never heard of generational wealth transfer calls.

Almost four years before she died, she was diagnosed with stage 4 cancer and given only six months to live. But then she ended up living three-and-a-half years, bleeding assets from the estate because she had no disability insurance and her health insurance was capped at one million dollars, not nearly enough. Soon she had to start spinning down the estate.

This was after her estate had already lost millions in accumulated wealth when the dot.com bubble popped spectacularly not long before her diagnosis. Looking at it after the fact, we felt her investment broker had over-invested in tech as he chased commission checks. Even worse, he didn't transfer money quickly enough to get her out when the market crashed.

My parents met at Louisville Dental College. They were great dentists, but very different in their financial approaches. My mother was frugal and tight with her money, saving on things she didn't need to replace, like computer systems. When she sold her clinic in 2005, she still had her original DOS software and dot matrix printers. My dad, on the other hand, was super tech-savvy, on the forefront of every change. They divorced when I was five; I always hoped they'd get back together when he left the military, not for marriage, but for a business partnership.

When they divorced, my dad moved to Germany and Belgium with the Air Force. My mom became a single parent of a toddler and a five-year-old. We had an 18 percent mortgage on our house, a car payment, student loan debt, and almost no discretionary income. Yes, she taught me tenacity and resourcefulness, but also to grow up very independently and very quickly because she was working all the time. I grew up fast when I was five.

We weren't deprived; she made sure we had decent clothes, had fun, and went out to eat—though it was only at "kids eat free" restaurants. I know what people mean when they say they don't have resources and can't get things done, but I feel there's always a way to see things through to completion without monetary resources as long as you have the drive and desire.

Your early years shape you. Now I'm a parent with four kids; my oldest is 17, and my youngest is eight. I try to show them ways to complete a task and get things done, and to see things through without relying on money as the crutch that's going to help you get there. We've seen crashes, even the 2007-08 housing market crash, where people were sure they were rich before they lost it all and had to start over. Think of the pandemic when people lost their businesses and all they'd poured into them. If you're relying on your ability to get things done because you have money, you're in for quite a surprise.

You need internal drive and discipline to really start moving the needle in your life. If you don't have those two essentials, you're *always* going to look for a crutch. If you do have them and you decide you're going to complete something, you'll find a way to complete it, even if it's not perfect. The drive for perfectionism hinders too many people; they don't even try for progress because they already hear inside their minds, *I can't do it perfectly so I'm not gonna try.*

NFL player Jerry Rice got to practice an hour early and stayed an hour late, just sprinting and catching footballs. His teammates said, "Jerry, you know how to catch a ball!" He'd say, "Yeah, but I'm trying to learn how to never drop it." He knew he wasn't perfect, and he wanted to be ready.

I loved football when I was in grade school and through seventh grade. I *loved* it even though I was the team runt. We moved to a ranch when I was in eighth grade, out of town, too far away for my always-working mom to ferry me home after practice at seven p.m. No more football. In ninth grade, I decided I *really* wanted to play baseball and told Mom, "If you're not going to take me, I'll stay at a friend's house." After two months of my spending half my time away, she realized I was serious and started showing up to practice and driving me home. I proved my point that if she wasn't going to help me do what I wanted to do, I'd do it without her.

Unfortunately, my baseball skills sucked. I was a great hitter in seventh grade but unable to hit anything in ninth grade. I could catch the ball, and I could throw, but not as far as the other players did. I was third string if that, but I'd said I was going to play and I tried my best. When my mom started showing up for games and saw I was warming the bench, she realized her error in making me quit football the year before. She was determined I'd sign up for football that year, but I explained if I couldn't measure up in baseball, I wasn't going to make it in football. She carried "mom guilt" around after she realized she'd forced me out of activities I'd really wanted.

> 66 You go fast when you're alone, but you go farther when you're a team, building a sense of purpose and mission 99

Being on the ranch was good for me in the long run, even if it prevented my high school sports career. When we moved out to the countryside, our dial-up internet kept me from staying online for extended periods because it tied up the only landline. The ways I filled my time—being with friends and reading tons of books—have become my lifelong passion. I learned to embrace being alone. Those years of learning never to be bored, spending time daydreaming and vision-casting, and living in my imagination, sent me up a better path. My career is built on helping other people build their vision and find ways to live. I can help them envision what they haven't been able to, and I can see their paths to reach it.

In my junior year, I went to Boy's State, where I met a diverse group including some West Point grads. For the first time I realized how out of shape I'd gotten. There I was, almost 17 years old, and while I wasn't fat, I was a chubby, tubby kid, not working out at all. One of the key lessons I learned at Boy State was the value of being in shape;

I realized I could get only so far with academics alone. Being there also fired up my pride in being an American. I come from a military background, and I began to see a possible future in the service.

That summer I applied to the Naval Academy. Those West Pointers inspired me, but not enough to apply to their school. I didn't want to go there. My mom was totally opposed to my going to the Naval Academy, and we debated why I should apply. Finally, it was so late she had to overnight my application, and she didn't stop reminding me how expensive the postage was, especially if I wasn't sure I was committed. In the next couple of months, I interviewed by U.S. Senators James Inhofe (R-OK) and Don Nickles (R-OK) as well as our Oklahoma congressman J.C. Watts (R-4th), and received nominations from all three for the Naval Academy. My application was lopsided, not well-balanced at all. I was strong in academics as the presumptive valedictorian with Boys' State and a few other awards and activities, but I lacked high school sports.

I heard nothing for months. A few weeks before graduation, we attended a school-wide assembly for the athletes and the scholarships they were being awarded. A navy captain showed up, gleaming in his dress whites, and as they were presenting the collegiate athletic scholarships, he presented me with a check made out to the Naval Academy for $300,000. Everybody went nuts.

My life changed when I went to the Naval Academy. Trust me, I'm glad I signed up sight unseen because I never would have gone if I had taken a site tour. When I arrived, I was feeling smug about my academics—I'd never had a B in my life! —until I went from a straight A to a C-D level student in no more than a heartbeat. I had no idea how to study or put in the work. It was harder than anything I was prepared to do in my life, and the first month there, I didn't think I'd make it. My mom sat me down and said, "If you're going to fail academically, just let me know now. Otherwise, I need to figure out why you're not trying."

Something clicked inside me. I knew I was trying, but I had a moment of introspection and asked myself, *Am I just going through the motions? I want to qualify for the economics route. I want to do mergers and acquisitions on Wall Street.* It became a defining moment because I realized I truly wanted to excel. I had to buckle down and retrain myself how to learn, how to build a strong work ethic. I'd never had to practice time management or really study beyond learning just enough to answer the questions. Now I began to absorb knowledge and context.

It was a tough first year, not just in academics. The Navy's physical training beat the crap out of me, which shouldn't have been a surprise, considering I'd spent four years being sedentary. I also needed to choose a sport, so I joined the crew team. I'd never seen a scull, I didn't even know how to move a boat, so I was trying to learn a brand-new sport from scratch, sleeping five or six hours a night, and getting PT every day. Don't forget the plebe year traditions where you are picked on endlessly as you try to learn rules and Navy traditions. *And* I was taking third-year calculus.

To me, graduating with honors in economics was a massive achievement, one of my proudest moments.

I took up a new sport in my mid-twenties and it's now one of my passions, both to play and to watch. I was 26, still in the Navy, teaching ROTC at University of Oklahoma and taking classes there for my MBA. Our home was 45 minutes from the campus so it didn't make sense to drive home to see my family for half an hour between classes and work.

I'd leave the campus in Norman, Oklahoma, drive to a nearby ice skating rink for an hour, and head to work. First, I learned to skate, then I bought gear and began learning to play hockey. It became my Sunday hobby, most definitely a full contact sport. I wasn't hurt at first but a few years later, playing beer league hockey in Nashville, I took a cross check and dislocated several lumbar vertebrae. Then I was 2 years into my financial planning journey, on 100 percent commission with no salary, and I was sidelined for a couple of months. I couldn't drive, couldn't move, and didn't earn money until after I had my surgery. (I still love the game!)

My time at the University of Oklahoma was pivotal in more ways than just hockey. My marriage was already on the rocks, and it weighed on me. I've learned in my life that I don't handle breaking up with people very well because I have an attachment issue. I'm more likely to say "Stick around and we'll figure it out," than make a clean break. I thought about my dad who spent years stationed on Air Force bases across the ocean. When he finally got out of the service, he didn't move back to Oklahoma. I was prepared to move to be near my two kids, but I was weighing the pros and cons of following them. I wondered how I could handle starting over if they moved again.

And then my dad, who lived in Tennessee, offered, "Move here. I'll help you grow your business." And so, within a six-week timeframe, I got divorced, got my MBA, and moved to Nashville, where I knew hardly anyone. Thankfully, I got some help in the beginning when my dad bought a couple of key policies he needed. That kept me in the game for the first couple of months.

Dad hadn't been a big part of my life while I was growing up, though we did visit him in Tennessee during the summers after he left the Air Force. Once I was at the Academy, he became a bigger part of my life. He was proud of what I was doing. He'd take a direct flight from Nashville and make the home football games at the Academy. When I was stationed in Hawaii, he flew out and took a Tiger Cruise, when the family came aboard for a few days. It does come down to family. I wanted to be closer to him, and my move to Nashville brought us together. Now we hang out, playing shuffleboard or bubble hockey at his house, watching football, and eating pizza. He does the grandfather thing with my four kids, Jason, Jessa, Justin, and John.

My history as a child of divorce influences my actions as a divorced father. I tell my kids I love them all the time because I didn't get many overt displays of affection when I was growing up. I knew I was loved, but it was not often said out loud. I'm much more verbal and demonstrative with my children.

My experience with my mother's estate and its multiple failures was the main reason for my new career trajectory. One of the key things I had learned from that debacle is to see what you start all the way through to completion, and to not look for the easy offramp. My grandfather taught me that, and he called it persevering until you succeed. I call it *getting through the suck*.

When I meet with my newly hired financial advisors, I tell them there's a guaranteed six-to-nine-month "window of the suck." No matter if you already have a million prospective contacts, eventually you'll run out of people you know to call, and you'll have to call someone you've never met before. (I'd run out of contacts a lot sooner than most.) That's when the suck really begins—finding ways to be comfortable when you're out of your comfort zone.

My business coach tells me I have a rescuer mentality and like to roll in as the White Knight. Unfortunately, that hasn't always turned out well. Two months into my new career, when I had absolutely no discretionary resources, I wrote a thousand-dollar check to keep a distant relative from being evicted. I took some precautions, of course, and made the check out to the landlord, but the person I was trying to help convinced a shady check-cashing company to give him the money. He'd sloppily crossed out the landlord's name, written in his own, and initialed the change in an attempt to copy my handwriting. He was out the door and buying drugs before the ink dried.

I was at work when I saw the check cleared and to whom. I got on the phone to the check-cashing company and yelled at them to give my money back, they'd fraudulently cashed the check, etc. I was more than a little hot under the collar. One of the managers walked through the bullpen at the time; he went straight to the supervising broker and said,

"Robinette is cussing out a client on the phone." It was obviously not a client, but I admittedly was using colorful language.

The supervising broker pulled me into his office, and snarled, "If you ever do that in my pit again, I'm firing you. You obviously think you're still in the military where you can do whatever you want," and then he cussed me out. The irony was not lost on me. Then I got an entire lecture on how I'm never going to make the cut, I hadn't passed any of the aptitude exams that predict who's going to be successful, and I should consider quitting. That was a major moment for me--all I need is someone telling me I can't do something. I thought, *Watch me!*

Revenge may have something to do with my success. Now, of the 7,500 agents in my brokerage group, I'm the number three financial planner in the nation, and I plan to become number one. Of the 120 insurance agents in our group, I'm number one for three years running.

About 18 months after I moved to Nashville, I won a "40 under 40 in Nashville" award from *Nashville Business Magazine* for outstanding talent and potential. I'd just turned 31; that award helped reassure me I'd made the right move.

Almost as soon as I got to town, I made time to work with a wide variety of charities. One of my favorites is Songs for Sound, where I've been on the board for about a decade. Its Hearoes program raises money for veterans suffering hearing loss. We launched an annual event called *All in for Vets Casino Night*, pick a different veterans' charity every year, and raise up to $40,000 to donate. I love that; I get great satisfaction, and the mission is deeply personal to me.

In a few cases, I've had regrets about diving into the wrong business partnerships. One of them was with a personal friend of mine, a private banker. He only wanted to do my clients' banking, he swore; he'd never dream of doing any planning or brokerage—none of the financial stuff *I* did. After I recommended him to my clients for banking purposes only, he changed to a bank that included wealth management and brought his entire list of clients with him to sell competing services and products.

Most people who provide a service go wide and network with everybody. I used to do that; I tried to give everyone their first deal. Now I've narrowed my reach and have gone deep with four or five partners and affiliates I trust and with whom I share clients. I don't worry about being pilfered anymore. I call my new system *Being the door versus being the room.* When I was trying to help everybody, I was the *room* where all these business associates came in; being the room meant I also was the overall controller, making sure everyone executed properly. When I go deeper with just a few close business relationships, I no longer have to worry about how these key partners implement their services because I know and trust them. Now I'm the *door* connecting them to me, and I'm just the overall connection. The format allows for more and better services for my clients.

Having a limited number of key relationships mattered even more when the pandemic hit. As the world shut down, we jumped into zooming without missing a beat and were able to talk through issues and plans from home.

A book I read years ago was probably one of the best and most helpful I've read and applied to my self-training. The author, whose name I unfortunately forget, wrote about how mountain climbers belay their ropes. They climb, attach an anchor point and clip in, and just keep going up. Even when they're doing it on their own and without a partner, the climber still anchors the rope. It's a slow, steady process. When they fall, it's only 5, 10, maybe 20 feet until anchors stop the fall, then they climb some more. If they don't set anchors and build in safeguards, when they fall it's to their death or destruction.

The author analyzes the difference between being *a failure* and *a fall-ure.* When you fall just a little bit, you have a minor interruption, a small fall-ure; you learned a lesson and can pivot and adjust. You didn't lose everything you've built. *You* are not a failure unless you neglect your safeguards.

Much of my thinking incorporates military leadership processes, where we run after-action reports after an incident. It's not to point blame, it's to analyze: *What went wrong? How do we overcome it? How do we adjust systems, processes, or procedures so things will run better?*

Every chance to screw up or fail at something is an opportunity to gain more experience and knowledge. You may have a slight setback and delay, but nothing's truly lost until you decide to pick up your puck and go home, saying, "Hey, I'm done. I quit. I'm out of here." I've developed the ability to watch how people act and retreat from things, then I ask, "How do you do it differently?" I don't fall into that trap of *Oh, we lost!* My thinking is *Well, why did we lose? What happens next? Where do we need to practice more?*

It's just brain science. We all live there in our neocortex, right in the front of our brain where all our logical modes operate. When we get stressed, cortisol is injected into our system and the whole logical part of our brain shuts down, emotions and fear take over, and our fight or flight response kicks in.

Learning how we respond to pressure has been very helpful and pivotal for me, especially over the last couple of years. You can't control what will happen or when. It's very easy to control how you **respond** to what happens. Too many people spiral into a doom loop and believe *everything always goes wrong* in their lives.

No! *Everything* doesn't *always* go wrong. If you believe that, you're constantly creating cortisol injections for yourself without practice or preparation on how to cope. When I coach new planners and agents fresh out of college and doing business for the first time, I start them with role playing. I tell them to start meeting people on Facebook, then ask the new virtual acquaintance for a 20-minute Zoom meeting to just talk.

My trainees ask in terror, "What am I going to sell the people I call?"

"Nothing," I grin. "You're gonna practice talking for the first time in your life while people wonder why you're on a call for 20 minutes. That alone will help you build better conversational skills and better ways to ask the right questions, so you actually focus and *listen* to what they're saying. It'll keep you from just blabbing away."

I think "shrinking time" is one of the greatest gifts you can give anyone. Whenever I can give someone a hand, I guide them to more clearly see where their future lies. Then I coach and encourage them along the path to reach a better version of that future. I also walk them through what I've done wrong on that path, and that helps shrink time on their journey. If I can take five years of you doing whatever it is you hate doing and shrink it down to six months, you'll have an additional four-and-a-half years of success you weren't going to have otherwise.

Early in my career, success was almost revenge, winning at all costs. As my career grew, success evolved to "I really *can* do what I put my mind to." (And what was that? Money.) As I have become much more prosperous, I don't measure success by my own successes, but by successful collaborations with others to find their vision, by teaching them how to become their version of success.

I've had to change the wording we use with clients because I want to be empathetic to all of their unique situations. I need to learn the vision *they* want to create before I can be their Sherpa, their guide, and go alongside them to help build their legacy. I never want to box them into something they may not want.

A lot of thought went into naming my firm, Lighthouse Planning. Using "lighthouse" in the name wasn't just a clever nautical theme to reflect on my background. A lighthouse is a serious thing; it lasts for generations, saving lives and ships in storms. Each lighthouse is unique; it's built on rocks, and only where there's invisible danger; it identifies where failure has already happened. Lighthouses help to prevent more failure—they're designed to prevent disasters.

Recently the entire firm had dinner together. I looked around our table: Our five financial planners, five staff members, interns, and significant others were drinking small-batch bourbon, eating tomahawk steaks and oysters, having a great end-of-year celebration. I thought back over the last 13 years, from the beginning when I thought I might not make it in my new career, to co-founding and eventually leaving my first firm, and then starting Lighthouse Planning at the end of 2019.

This company was created by returning to the ethos of the military, building a sense of purpose and mission: *You go fast when you're alone, but you go farther when you're a team.* We've attracted an amazing group who want to work at the firm, serve our clients, build, and grow.

Instead of a rah-rah end-of-year speech, my talk to my team expressed my thanks. When we started, I'd had no idea how big we would become. I'm grateful with where things are, so much so, that if we didn't add another client, I would still consider our firm to be a massive success. I can sit in appreciation of the abundance and happiness we have right now, while at the same time I know my team. I'm confident enough in their culture and ethics that I believe we will reach new levels of achievement and success, even better, faster, and easier.

We're not done yet.

ABOUT CHRIS ROBINETTE

Chris was a young U.S. Navy officer heading to deployment in the North Arabian Gulf when his mother died, frustrated because he couldn't immediately head home and help his teenage sister and grandparents follow his mother's wishes. Seeing the consequences and costs of her estate plan being overridden and ignored after her death, he realized the vital importance of solid financial planning and building a lasting legacy.

Since he began his financial planning career in 2011, and especially since he founded Lighthouse Planning in 2019, he helps his clients avoid the sudden loss and shock his family experienced. He assists them as they envision and reach their goals and grow their legacies to maximize their impact to their family, community, and philanthropic plans.

Chris is generous with his knowledge, coaching others through their mindset and leadership development journeys beyond just the financial as he continued to find ways to help them grow and find ways to make a meaningful impact in life.

He is passionate about serving his community, donating time, energy, and money to many nonprofits, and hosting an annual casino night to raise money for a variety of veterans' charities.

Born and raised near Oklahoma City, Oklahoma, Chris graduated from the U.S. Naval Academy, where he earned a B.S. in Economics with honors, and the University of Oklahoma, where he earned an M.B.A. Chris moved to Nashville in 2011, where he's recognized as a top business leader. Awards include Nashville 40 Under Forty (2013), Veteran Business Leader (2015), and Forbes List for TN (2024, 2025, 2026).

He enjoys cheering on the local National Hockey Association team, the Nashville Predators, and spends time with his four children.

Chris' message is, *Stand tall and be the example for others. You are the lighthouse in the storm guiding others home safely.*

 LHPLANNING.com

 https://www.instagram.com/chrisrobinette04

 https://www.facebook.com/chrisrobinette04

 https://www.linkedin.com/in/crobin04

Heal the World with the Impact Healing Movement

MARKITA BROOKS

'm a healer, though not a medical healer nor the kind of healer who redirects energy. My gift is healing souls.

Since I was a young girl, I've known God put me on earth for an important purpose. My mother prayed for a child, and when I was born, God told her to protect me, that He had plans to use me.

Though I've experienced a lot of trauma and pain in this short life of mine, you wouldn't know it to look at me. Why? Because God taught me to bring my soul to Him for daily healing. Because I'm so spiritually sensitive, I can't work when my soul is broken. Out of sheer necessity, my soul has been the focus of my journey with God.

What He does to my soul is like automobile maintenance. Just as a car needs regular service if it's going to operate effectively, my soul needs regular maintenance or I'll shut down. To be useful in the lives of others, without being damaged by their challenges or damaging them by my own challenges, requires my soul to be intact, *all* the time.

I'm also an overachiever, pushing my limits and stretching myself thin. So, in addition to maintenance, I also need recharging. That's why each morning I spend two to three hours in God's Presence, allowing

Him to heal what's hurting, transform my thinking, speak truth to my heart and refresh me for the day ahead. I also pray for others to be healed and for regions of the world to be transformed. Being an entrepreneur affords me the flexibility to structure my time, a luxury I need to respond to direction and interruptions from God throughout the day. These encounters provide revelation, strategy and innovation that have made my businesses successful and my ministries relevant.

However, it hasn't always been this way. Let me take you on a little journey through my healing and transformation. Hopefully by the end of it, you'll want to join me in my Impact Healing Movement to receive your own inner healing and the empowerment to lead transformationally as we impact nations together.

You can only be healed deeply by making the journey to the other side of truth. The truth is not always comfortable. Sometimes it's painful. Sometimes it's messy. Sometimes it reveals things we would rather avoid. But healing does not come through avoidance. It comes when we have the courage to look directly at what is true—without denial, without self-protection, and without rushing to fix it. Truth creates space for God's voice to be heard. And in that space, healing flows. Peace settles. Wholeness begins.

This is shalom—not the absence of difficulty, but the presence of peace, rest, and alignment in the midst of it. Have courage today. Truth is not your enemy. Truth is the doorway to healing.

My parents, Michael and Stella Boney, are amazing singers, and I wanted to become a singer just like them when I grew up. Listening to their duets was a delight, and if they were dancing together in the living room, all was well with the world—my world at least.

Then, my world fell apart. Their passionate love became volatile, with unpredictable ups and downs that threatened the stability I relied on. There would be a blowup and my dad would leave or he'd pack a duffel bag in the wee hours of the morning to avoid a conflict. Though my parents would reconcile and be "in love" again sometime later, every new breakup damaged all three of us a bit more until the day Dad left for good. My mother stopped singing, and she and I were both devastated.

When I learned I could excel at almost everything I put my mind to, I decided to put my mind to a lot of things. I wanted to create a life that would bring singing and dancing back into my house. I wanted to experience the sense of safety and shalom that I had as a child, before my dad left. My mother told me my priorities in life should be God, my family and getting a good education, and I listened. I always knew I'd go to college, so I was focused on becoming the type of student colleges would want. My schoolwork and extracurricular activities positioned me to be accepted by all the schools to which I applied, and I was offered 50 academic scholarships.

Working hard was a great distraction from the pain in my soul, though I wasn't distracted every moment. There were times that I would write dark poetry to express some of my pain. I kept a box with items that all represented something that had damaged me over the years. Other times, I even contemplated suicide. No one at school or among my friends suspected anything was wrong with me, but my mother knew.

As an introvert, I tried to keep my pain to myself, even when I was molested by a guidance counselor in middle school and attacked by a boyfriend in high school. I couldn't hide my pain well enough to fool my mother, and she took me to a therapist who encouraged her to make sure I talked; my therapist said I would eventually explode emotionally if I kept everything bottled up.

My mother did just that; she sat me down routinely and asked me pointed questions about what was going on in my life. When I was younger, it was really helpful, but as I got older, I perfected my ability to hide the pain that was there under the surface.

Now, as a minister and coach, I can tell when people aren't being completely open, when they're not sharing what really matters to them. While I'm patient, I'm also honest about the benefits of release and the pain of suppression. I learned that lesson the hard way.

During my college years, I experienced a few personal traumas that I did my best to suppress. The summer after my freshman year, I was raped by a friend I'd known since middle school. Other than allowing myself to cry for a day, I pretended the rape never happened. I went back to school in the fall and buried myself in activities: I led the University of Richmond Multicultural Student Union (MSU) as President, continued to lead Ngoma, the African dance company I'd started the previous year, and pledged a sorority. It was a year of life-changing distractions. I will never forget the people I met, many of whom are still vital in my life, like my line sisters who pledged the sorority with me. I will never forget the programs and events I put on for MSU and Ngoma. And I will never forget what I did to my soul to get through that year of pretending I had not been attacked.

While I still denied to myself that I had been raped, I decided to never be a victim again. During my sophomore year, I chose who I was going to date and for how long. When I was done with them, I disposed of them. I had become the predator, convinced this would protect me from ever being someone's prey again. What I didn't realize was that vow I made to myself to never again be a victim caused me to victimize myself. I was treating myself like an object, just as my attacker had done.

The damage was done by my junior year, and I was burned out. I was done. Done trying to be the best student. Done trying to smile and pretend. Done with having the casual, predatory relationships that I used to try to fill the hole in my soul. Done with so many activities and responsibilities. Done with caring about my grades. I decided to discover *myself*, to delve into what *I* needed.

My season of self-discovery was short but important because it prepared me for the next season of my life, the time when I finally made room for God. I created a rite of passage for myself, which included spending time alone with Him. I needed Him to answer some questions for me about my identity and future. While I asked questions of Him, He began to pose questions to me.

The Lord revealed to me that I *had* been raped the summer after my freshman year in college. I had been denying what happened to me during the attack because the rapist had been my friend and I had agreed to go into his bedroom. I'd been denying the truth: My attempts at refusal, all my terrified cries of *NO!* did make what happened actual rape, not a consensual experience. I remembered how angry he became at every "no" and how his face became threatening. He was no longer the friend I had known all those years, but someone entirely different and terrifying.

> "Our souls yearn for what we are designed to do."

When I spent time alone with God to discuss my identity and future, He revealed that I didn't see myself as precious. Instead, I was using my body and damaging my soul to keep from seeing the truth: I had been violated. And not just my body was violated—so were my soul and trust.

I realized I should be in a committed relationship, not casual ones, and made a point of finding a serious boyfriend, though I still hadn't discovered my value or the value of a covenant love relationship. When I decided my boyfriend didn't value me the way I deserved to be valued, I rebounded and married someone else—Sam, a friend from my past who did value me.

My family had known Sam for years and loved him, but they knew we weren't ready for marriage. I married him against the wise counsel of my family and without consulting God in prayer. Deciding to marry was my own solution to the problem God had pointed out. I had not yet learned that when the Lord reveals you have a problem, He wants to be involved in the solution.

At that time, I was working for an insurance company in Philadelphia, Pennsylvania, about six hours from my hometown of Hampton, Virginia. Sam and I thought it would be a good city for a young couple wanting to explore the world. Originally, I had accepted a position as a change agent with an international consulting company in Philly. I looked forward to traveling all over the world to work with business clients, and Sam planned to travel with me. Yet right before our wedding, I discovered I was three months pregnant, and constant international travel looked a bit less appealing. I switched to a position that would allow us to establish roots as a family, because it didn't require travel.

Marriage and motherhood entered my life at the same time and not according to my best-laid plans. During my second trimester, my entire body became swollen. I showed my huge, puffy ankles and feet to my obstetrician and explained I couldn't wear my shoes anymore. I knew this was a bad sign, but my doctor wouldn't listen to me. He was dismissive and just told me not to worry and wear slippers instead.

A few days later, I was reading a pregnancy calendar, and it warned that swelling and seeing squiggly lines could be symptoms of preeclampsia (toxemia), a life-threatening complication of pregnancy. I had both symptoms! My mother rushed me to the emergency room, an obstetrician was called in to check me over, and I was immediately admitted to the hospital. The doctor who saw me was a woman, and I'm convinced God used her to help save my life. She understood the seriousness of my condition and made sure everyone around me, including my regular obstetrician, did as well.

A few days later, my blood pressure spiked so high that I became blind. The medicine they were administering through the IV caused me to go in and out of consciousness with vivid dreams. One morning, a new doctor came into the room. I couldn't see him, but he had a French accent. So, in my mind, he became Gerard Depardieu, the French actor. "Gerard" began to talk to me about my baby, but I thought it was a dream and ignored him until my mother told me I needed to listen. He repeated, "I'm the neonatal surgeon. After we take the baby, I'm going to bring the baby directly into our neonatal unit, which is one of the best in the nation."

"Take the baby"? The team of doctors assigned to my care were planning to induce labor, but no one had told me. When I inquired, another doctor explained that my body had been fighting my daughter as though she was a parasite. After she was delivered, he said, my systems should go back to normal, including my vision.

They tried to induce labor, which was terribly painful, but my cervix would not dilate, so they performed an emergency Caesarean section on me. My daughter Samaria was born almost three months early, just as I reached the 28th week of my pregnancy, and she weighed exactly two pounds. I could not see her at first, but when my vision was restored a few days later, I was greeted by this beautiful, tiny brown baby with a head full of silky black hair.

Nurses wheeled me into the neonatal unit to do "kangaroo care" with Samaria; they laid her against my bare skin, which helped to regulate her temperature and stabilize her heart rate. I wasn't planning to breastfeed, but when they explained my milk could increase her chances of survival, I did so willingly. She was too premature to be able to latch on to my breast, so I pumped milk that was fed through a tube in her nose.

After a few days, I was sent home. I went into that hospital with a baby in my belly, and for six months, she'd been my best friend as I went to work and moved through my day. Leaving the hospital without her, I felt terribly empty.

At home, I was on bed rest and unable to visit Samaria. I spent most of my maternity leave in bed, but the time was not wasted. I spent every day praying fervently for God to spare her life and heal her completely. When I was finally released from bed rest, I drove myself to the hospital to see Samaria. After a full two months, she was breathing well on her own and was released from the hospital, one month before her original due date.

She came home to me, wearing a heart monitor. A week later, I had to go back to work because my maternity leave was over. Daycare facilities don't accept babies on heart monitors, so my mom quit her job to take care of Samaria, and my father helped us financially while she wasn't working.

My mother took excellent care of Samaria, and God healed her completely. At her next check-up, she was so big and healthy that the pediatrician couldn't believe she was a preemie. He took her off the heart monitor and all her medications. God is a healer, and He heals us completely,

As the 21-year-old parent of a preemie, I was growing up fast. I had a lot of responsibilities on my plate—a new career, adjusting to my post-college adult life, caring for a baby, plus learning to live with my husband who had even more growing up to do than I did. Everything was non-negotiable except that last part, so I asked Sam to move out.

Had I focused less on my situation and more on God's power, I would have trusted God with our marriage, and I would not have asked Sam to leave, but God works all things together for our good, even our bad decisions. Now, I'm married to the love of my life and partner in all things, Hassan Brooks, who has a very special relationship with Samaria that's a blessing to them both.

After Sam and I separated, I planned to move back home to Virginia to be near my family. I gave notice at my job in Philadelphia because I knew God would provide for us in Virginia. I didn't know how He would do it, but I had faith. When I went home for a few interviews, I stopped by a youth development agency, a firm I'd worked for when I was younger, just to say "hi" to the staff. They had sponsored many of the clubs and programs I was involved with during my school years, and I had my first job working on their youth staff.

The agency had an opening for a Youth Development Director and invited me to apply. The hiring process was intriguing; both adults and young people interviewed me and many other applicants. I learned after the fact that the adults asked the teens for recommendations, and I was hired because the young people chose me. As a Youth Development Director, I later supervised my own youth staff at the agency, creating fond memories I cherish to this day.

Though I worked in Hampton, I decided to live in Virginia Beach, about an hour away. I have family there, and I wanted my daughter to grow up around her cousins. I put everything I had into my job and was being groomed to become the Executive Director eventually. I had a corner office, I was writing curricula and I was the statewide coordinator of a sexual and physical violence prevention program. Then I plateaued. I felt I had gone as far as I could creatively. From the outside, it seemed as though everything was falling in place for me, but I knew something was missing, and I wanted more.

Unrest and dissatisfaction are excellent indicators that it's time to go to the next level, especially when everything seems "fine" otherwise. Our souls yearn for what we are designed to do in every area of life. I'm a mother. I was spending too many hours away from my daughter and regretted that she was being raised by other people. I'm an innovator, and though I was doing creative work, there was more for me to create, to build.

I will never forget that day, March 13, 2001. It was about 9 p.m., and I was sitting on the toilet, trying to find a private place to catch my breath and have a moment alone. Samaria and I had been home for about an hour after I picked her up from daycare in Hampton. Perched on my humble throne, I had an epiphany: It was time for a major change. I needed to move on from the agency where I worked. I needed to do what was in my heart. So, I cried out to God for guidance. *There must be more than this!*

Let me warn you, crying out to God invites Him into your situation, which is why we cry out. However, when He shows up, He may reveal things He's been saying for a long time, but we were not in a spiritual position to hear. That night He said to me, *The Truth In The Spirit.* What? What is that? Could this possibly be the name of my own youth development agency?

As I began to write out plans and put legalities in place, everyone said to me, "What you're planning sounds like a ministry." I vehemently objected and shut that down each time. Ministry? I'm not a minister. I'm a youth worker. That's what *I* thought at the time.

While I worked on my business plan, God put it in my heart to go on a truth journey instead. He said, "If you're going to start The Truth In The Spirit, you need to know what truth is." That sounded logical, so I agreed. What a can of worms I opened up!

On the journey, I learned the truth is objective, not subjective. It's absolute, complete. Partial truth is not truth at all. And the truth has a form, an existence, and a name—Yeshua. That's Jesus' Name in the original Hebrew. He said of Himself that He is the Way, the Truth, and the Life. As I began to search for truth, I found Him in an intimate and glorious way.

I also found out the truth about myself. He revealed to me many of the malfunctions in my soul, the imperfect actions I do because of trauma. He made clear to me that I had not been truly living but *surviving.* He called me to become ME—the me He designed, not the one my pain had created. I wasn't sure I even knew this person, but I tried to remember who I was as a young child. I figured that would give me some clues.

As I began walking out this truth journey with the Lord, He led me back to His Word. I hadn't read the Bible consistently in years. But now, as I searched for truth, it became one of my favorite books. In the Scriptures, I discovered the truth about God, myself, the world, and just about every topic under the sun. It was an exciting experience because the Lord led me to read chapters each morning that revealed some truth I would need that day. The Word of God came alive for me! He then began to speak to me through His Word.

Later, He called me to be His prophet. I asked Him seriously, "You still make those?" I thought, *What do I know about speaking on behalf of God?* He, Himself, taught me what being a prophet meant. Not only did He teach me to hear from Him and to speak to others on His behalf, but He gave me His heart about people and the world, so that even my tone, my walk, reflected Him. Yet, it was distinctly ME—the me that He designed.

One of the first instructions He gave me as His prophet was to quit my job at the youth agency. I was becoming stifled by the job but it was going relatively well, giving me a sense of security and paying my bills. Of course, I asked for confirmation of His will, which He provided in no uncertain terms. Then, I put in my three-week notice. God was not calling me to another job. He was calling me to give up everything to follow Him.

Now, most people will not be called by God to quit their jobs, though a lot of people fear that is exactly what will happen if they get close to Him. For me, He was delivering me from dependence upon a paycheck, health insurance, and a 401(k) to become the entrepreneur and innovator I'm designed to be. He also drew me away from everything that would distract me from Him, for a season, so that He could make me over.

He had to. I had made so many vows to myself about what I would and wouldn't do and how I would live that I had limited myself. My growth was stifled by ME. I was too busy being responsible. Don't get me wrong, I value responsibility, but when it becomes a crippling obligation, it can be destructive.

I was slow to recognize that I had invited God to intervene in my life well before I cried out to Him on March 13th. The beautiful little person living with me was watching everything I did. She sang the songs I listened to and danced to the videos I watched. As I began to realize this, I started to change, to be a better model for her and expose her to different influences. If it was inappropriate for her, it became inappropriate for *us*. I changed my music and entertainment to include versions that welcomed God, because I knew they would always be appropriate. Changing what I watched and listened to made positive changes to my heart as well, and when I felt dissatisfied, His Spirit, residing within me, called out to Him.

Because of my abandonment issues, I craved security, so I'd never considered building my own enterprises. Though I'm designed to be a risk-taker and to freely innovate, the fears that had been controlling me put a lid on my innate impulses. Once God healed me, He was able to free my thinking to consider the possibilities and take risks. Now, I live by faith, a gift from God, and it activates other gifts within me. Those gifts have created multiple ministries and businesses, while helping other people discover their true identities and fulfill their real dreams. And now I receive paychecks and have health insurance and a 401(k) through my own enterprises.

We need to discover what lies beneath our fears, our sense of duty, and the programming that's been layered over our true selves. Only then can we make a lasting mark on the world around us that will leave a legacy we're proud to claim. That is the legacy I want to leave for my children, Samaria and Joshua.

The Truth In The Spirit has become a vibrant international ministry; through it, I'm able to help individuals, communities, and other ministries discover the Truth and flow in the Spirit, leading to cooperation and lasting transformation.

Through Kingdom Wealth, LLC, my Bible-based business coaching firm, I help people bring their visions into reality and propel them to their next level. This growth and change happens through business coaching but also the intense healing they receive through coaching sessions with me. My coaching clients agree that the healing aspect of Kingdom Wealth has been essential to their success.

> Now I live by faith, a gift from God.

Through Congregation Or Shalom, which I lead with my husband, Messianic Rabbi Hassan Brooks, we shine God's light into darkness, establishing peace and wholeness in our region. My various other enterprises, books, and community involvements connect me with amazing people who are also interested in making a positive difference in this world, which we do together.

I want to invite you to join us in healing the world by starting with your own inner healing. I've started a movement—the Impact Healing Movement. Our focus is facilitating deep inner healing, empowering transformational leaders, and impacting whole nations. It's time for something real and lasting. We've had enough surface talk that skirts the real issues, enough projects that only make a dent in problems. The world is ready for healing that transforms lives and impacts nations.

When individuals are healed, they're empowered to effectively cooperate toward positive change. Solutions arise from that collaboration to address oppression, degradation, and the world's worst problems. When people are healed, they abandon destructive behaviors and employ constructive ones. That is true for whole systems in every nation throughout the world. I know, because when I was broken, I brought pain to others around me. Yet, when God healed me, He began to use me in the healing of others and whole regions. My strengths now focus on innovation rather than degradation.

This is what the Impact Healing Movement is all about, both for individuals and whole nations. Business innovation, financial wisdom, creative systems, strategic infrastructure, empowering education, and much more all flow from healed individuals working together to transform a region. Every gift and discipline is needed to address real challenges with healed hearts. You are what's missing in the world. Receive your inner healing and join me in healing the world through the Impact Healing Movement.

ABOUT MARKITA BROOKS

Markita Brooks is multi-talented, family-oriented, and incredibly busy, showing people and organizations how to make and manage money in ethical and God-centric ways.

Her religious and community involvement is anchored by The Truth in The Spirit, which she founded and for which she serves as ministry leader, focused on transformation and empowerment for individuals, ministries, businesses and communities. With her husband Hassan, she leads Congregation Or Shalom, a Messianic Jewish temple in Richmond, Virginia.

She is founder and chief executive officer of Kingdom Wealth LLC, a Bible-based business coaching firm, as well as founder and president of the Ari Network Inc., a global network connecting Kingdom entrepreneurs. She founded and leads the Company of Apostles and Prophets, the Ecclesia Network of Ministries, the Nehemiah Network of business owners, the Invitation Movement, and the National Kingdom Council. She consults and trains pastors and leaders in many organizations and ministries worldwide.

Markita is also involved in secular business as the Class-A contractor and co-owner of a successful construction corporation and is a business consultant. She serves on seven nonprofit boards of directors, and serves on the Minority Policy Priorities Task Force of the Financial Services Innovation Coalition, the Leadership Team for the Fairfield Family Circle (uniting descendants of slaves and enslavers to heal and move beyond the legacy of enslavement), and as the Vice Delegate for the USA to the United Nations for Israel (UNIFY).

Her degree in leadership studies from the University of Richmond was just the beginning of her education. She has also been trained through Kad-Esh MAP Ministry's Global Revival Messianic Apostolic Prophetic Bible School and the Messianic Yeshiva of the International Alliance of Messianic Congregations and Synagogues.

The author of *The Road to Damascus: Transformation for the Next Level* and *5 Biblical Keys to Unlocking Wealth*, Markita gives motivational speeches internationally. She also finds valuable time for her husband Hassan, her children Joshua and Samaria, and her grandchildren.

 markitabrooks.com

 truthservices.org

 kingdomwealthllc.com

It's My Turn to Be The Lighthouse

DAINE PATTON

Though I never thought I'd grow up to be a lighthouse, guiding people in their personal development and careers, that's where I find myself today. I'm grateful to be able to share how I developed the mindset that has made me successful.

My unlikely route to success began when I was given my first responsible job at age twelve. The pay was nonexistent, but the responsibility was consequential: I was entrusted with the care of my eight-year-old brother at night when my hard-working, hard-partying parents went out for some fun. Almost two nights a week for the next few years, I did a good job taking care of Levi. We are a loving family, and I never felt the extra responsibility was unfair.

Those early years built the underpinnings of my life's purpose: feeling responsible for others, knowing I need to help them, all while doing it happily and as well as I can. I'm grateful, too, for the grounding those years gave me. My attitude was positive and I never really begrudged caring for my brother. Still, I wasn't perfect, and I sometimes resented how my teenage social life was curtailed.

When I turned sixteen, I handed Levi's care back to my parents and began to earn money. My mom, dad, and brother adapted to the new arrangement without a hitch. Levi was twelve by then and a great guitarist; he just went along with my parents and played open stages at their favorite bars. It was the start of his successful career as a professional musician.

Though I no longer took care of Levi, I still had responsibility for kids (a lot of them!) at my new job, because I worked in a family fun center. Overseeing the safety and happiness of children and young teens was at the top of my job description for the next six years.

My parents passed their work ethic to me; I was always willing to learn new tasks and work hard. My bosses noticed and appreciated my actions and behavior, and I was given more responsibility. In my sophomore year, I quit the football team to work longer hours, and after two years on the job, I had hopes of becoming assistant manager. But one hot day I decided to chop the sleeves off my official logoed work T-shirt and let the breeze cool my arms (and show off my muscles). Two years of being a model employee didn't keep me from being canned.

Being fired turned out to be a blessing in disguise, because I went to work for Shauna, the manager of a laser tag center. She saw my potential, loved my great attitude and my open mindset, and encouraged me to take on more responsibility. She was a much better manager, by far, than my previous boss, and I've emulated her management style for twenty years. She empowered me, never reprimanded me, and treated me like a competent adult *which* helped me keep my mindset in a growth mode. In return, I always tried to make her look good to her bosses and other staff members.

Shauna became my first mentor, and for the next two years I thrived. Besides teaching me business basics—how to hire, schedule, train, supervise, and keep records—she explained how things worked and why. She promoted me to assistant manager, encouraged me to develop my fledgling management instincts, invited my input into marketing techniques as well as work procedures, and listened to and sometimes adopted my suggestions. She was one of those rare, excellent bosses who always give kudos when they're earned. She passed on my good deeds and ideas to Scott, the regional manager of the international corporation we worked for, and she never took credit for what I did or suggested. By the time I was 19 years old, Shauna had taught me most of the managerial skills I still use today.

The years between my 19th and 21st birthdays were pivotal ones for me. A lot happened in just a sliver of time: I became a father, moved from my hometown of Lincoln, Nebraska, to Oklahoma City, was promoted to manager of an underperforming laser tag center, and succeeded beyond corporate expectations.

Let's break it down step by step.

When my girlfriend, Mandy, realized she was pregnant, she was 18 and I was barely 19. We knew we wanted the baby, but we weren't ready to get married. She finished high school and we moved into an apartment, and in December, our son Charlie was born. I was crazy about Charlie from the moment he arrived and was determined to be a big part of his life, no matter how Mandy and I ended up. He was the most important member of our young family, and I wasn't about to let him go.

A few months later, right around my 20th birthday, Scott said, "You have the energy I need and want," and he offered me a promotion as manager of another laser tag center plus a 50 percent raise to $30,000 a year. The kicker was the arcade was 400 miles away in another state, one I'd never visited and where I knew nobody. To me, it was the chance of a lifetime and I had no doubts. The money was a fortune to me two full decades ago, and the opportunity was better than I'd hoped for.

I didn't wait to talk about the offer with Mandy, which in retrospect was not the smartest or kindest move. I grabbed the job with both hands and rushed home to tell her we would be leaving town in a month. I was sure I was on the trajectory to success, and I wasn't about to let the opportunity get away from me.

Excited and raring to prove myself, I moved to Oklahoma City with a new baby and a lonely and resentful teenage girlfriend. We didn't know a soul in town, and we didn't have any plans to develop a social life. I was there to focus on work, and I wasn't worried about Mandy being able to cope. In my 20-year-old ignorance, I assumed she'd find some other young mothers and be happy. I didn't realize how badly she needed a support system.

I inherited two assistant managers; both were older and had hoped for the manager's job. It took some doing for me to win them over and have them see me as a viable boss. I used the techniques I'd learned from Shauna, empowering them, giving them credit, listening to them, and mentoring them. We began to put the laser tag on track to double the business.

From the start, I went above and beyond in my new management role. I had a lot to prove besides my obvious loyalty. My mantra was *How can we make more money and give our customers a better experience?* (I still think that way today.) To me, it's common sense, but unfortunately, it's not that common. I did my best to make my mindset and my attitude contagious.

In one year, we doubled the gross revenue to $1 million, and the arcade was succeeding beyond the corporation's goals. I saw myself on the fast track to success with this international corporation, and I celebrated my 21st birthday with my first beer and a lot of hope for the future.

Unfortunately, work was the only place I was succeeding. I came home exhausted each night—wound-up and needing to decompress. I was miserable company, not communicative or supportive. Mandy was unhappy being at home 24/7 with Charlie, without her family, friends, or any help or parenting guidance. She knew she didn't want to continue along this lonely path, and she became focused on going to college. My raise paid the bills for our family of three, but we were living paycheck to paycheck. I couldn't see how college could happen without Mandy also taking on a part-time job to help pay for childcare and tuition costs. She didn't believe a work option was feasible, much less desirable.

After a year of misery in a strange town, Mandy announced she was moving back home with our Charlie to live with her parents and go to college.

> As much as I loved my job, I loved my son more.

As much as I loved my job, I loved my son more. I barely hesitated. In just one month, I extricated myself from the lease and the job and followed Charlie back to Lincoln, unemployed but determined to be in my son's life, whatever it took.

Shauna, my former boss and mentor, had moved on and there was a new general manager in place at the arcade where I'd worked before. The only position available was my old assistant manager position. I took it gratefully, rented a place for myself, and began to take care of Charlie every chance I could.

Mandy became involved in college classes and social life, our roles reversed, and she handed Charlie over to me. I could afford daycare, but often my hours at the center included evenings and weekends. My parents pitched in with babysitting or I wouldn't have been able to cope.

My attitude was flagging for the first time in my life; I resented taking care of other people's children at night when *I* wanted to care for Charlie. I realized having an eight-to-five job would be the only way I could handle being a single dad.

In high school, I had thought about becoming a lawyer. As a good but not top-ranked student, I probably wouldn't have qualified for an

academic scholarship. Fortunately, I had been a good enough football player to receive a college recruitment letter. I derailed my potential for an athletic scholarship when I quit football to work more hours. At work I had regular promotions and salary increases, and by the time I was 18 I was earning decent money.

When it was time to make a decision about college, I thought about all the years I'd have to commit to studying for a law degree, and working won out over school. There wasn't much pushback from my parents; nobody in my family had attended college and it wasn't automatically expected of me.

Now I was 21, the sole support of a son, and I'd run into a wall looking for a job. With no college under my belt, my options were limited, and that wall looked high.

Construction work was always one of those options, but I knew enough about the trades to realize it wasn't what I wanted. My dad had always been in construction, and I saw the toll it'd taken on his body. I had worked with him occasionally when I was younger, and my experience reinforced my dislike for construction work.

I continued working at the center for months as I searched for a new job and finally found a position doing termite control for a national firm. The job had regular hours, decent pay, and the work was interesting. Once I learned the technical aspects of the job, I appreciated the autonomy I had in dealing with clients, especially with solving problems. I was working outside, listening to podcasts and music, with a tremendous amount of freedom. My attitude rebounded and Charlie and I were thriving.

Once I'd mastered the intricacies of termite control, I started training for animal pest control. That was a different job entirely, and I soon realized the downside. The one thing mice, ants, roaches, and spiders had in common was the poison I used to kill them. I was drenched in toxicity every day, and I had to strip down outside the house and shower before I could touch Charlie.

There must be something better than poison, for the animals at least, I thought almost every day. My routes brought me back to most customers each month, and like clockwork, the mice had used the same cracks and holes to find their way back into the house. I'd learned enough construction fundamentals from my dad to find how they got inside and I had the skills to fill them in and block their passage. I started fixing the holes, though it wasn't part of our services. Unfortunately, my skills worked all too well. My customers no longer needed monthly rodent control services and my route dwindled.

We had referred most critter-infested customers to a small local firm that specialized in wildlife control and abatement. I went to my boss and suggested we add this service to our business instead of giving the work away and was thrilled when he agreed. Soon, I was responsible for dealing with bats, rats, snakes, and assorted other animals. Best of all, I truly enjoyed taking care of people's animal infestation problems. Poison wasn't involved and in most cases we didn't need to kill the animals. Prevention and removal was better for the animals and for the environment, to say nothing of my own body.

Life was settling into a comfortable pattern for Charlie and me, especially after I bought a house for the two of us, but something was missing. It'd been four years since I'd had a partner, and more years than I liked to remember since I'd dated anyone. When Charlie visited his mom, the evenings were particularly long and lonely. I realized I was finally ready to find someone to be in my life.

One of my cousins suggested Plenty of Fish, a computer dating app, and he said it was a relatively stressless way to meet compatible women. It may have been stressless for most guys, but it was a hair-raising eye-opener to me. I'd never dated adult women, and I quickly learned they were very different from the young girls I'd known before my dating career ended at 18. Six years later when I dove back into the dating pool, I was no more sophisticated than I'd been back then. I didn't want one-night stands, but these women were bold. I was dumbfounded and shocked by some of the messages they sent me.

As I scrolled through my potential matches, I was intrigued by Lena, a cute blonde with a degree in early childhood education. She owned her own business, running a day care out of her home, and she seemed mature in a way that made me comfortable. We talked for weeks, and when we finally met in person, I fell for her, hard. Fortunately, so did my son. Since Charlie and I were a package deal, when the time came we proposed to Lena together. We were married in 2011, and Charlie's younger brothers, Harvey and Franklin, joined the family in 2013 and 2016, respectively.

My bosses appreciated the work I was doing and expanded the division by buying my competition. The two employees who came along with the sale taught me advanced trapping and exclusion techniques before they moved on. I was happy, in control of the wildlife control work and training new employees.

As our family grew, Lena and I started thinking about finding a larger home. We knew we needed more income to afford a bigger house, and we realized my income wasn't increasing along with the wildlife division's profits. I may have been "appreciated," but I had to ask for every increase I got. I began to resent having to justify getting a raise, but because I needed the money for the house, I went in and made my case.

Yes, I received the raise, but my bosses attached unreasonable demands. They insisted we charge considerably more for the work. Worse, they also demanded we convince our clients to pay for unnecessary services and threaten dire consequences if they didn't sign up. I saw myself as a steward of wildlife, someone who educated clients and solved problems, not someone who'd scare them into paying for something they didn't need.

Price gouging and fear mongering are morally wrong in my book. I fought back and argued with my bosses but got nowhere. Before things became unbearable, Lena suggested I leave and open my own wildlife control business. She made a good point; I had four years of wildlife abatement experience by this time and owned much of the equipment I'd need to get started.

> Price gouging and fear mongering are morally wrong

It didn't take much to make me realize I was ready for the next step. After giving my employers two months' notice, I opened Bats to Rats Wildlife Control and Prevention in early 2015.

One of the key things I knew about being a small business owner was the need to network. Almost as soon as *Bats to Rats* was painted on my truck, I joined Business Networking International (BNI), an organization that helps members through training and referrals as well as networking. I enjoyed meeting other small business owners in Lincoln and began volunteering for a variety of responsibilities. By the time three years had passed, I'd moved from membership committee to group president to Nebraska's BNI Member of the Year. Lena and I were sent to represent the state at BNI's International Conference in Long Beach, California. It was an honor, and also a badly needed break for the two of us.

I joined other professional community groups, volunteering, networking, getting some coaching, and beginning to coach others. This was the start of my personal development work. The time I was spending squeezed my work responsibilities, because I was still the only employee. I realized I needed to work smarter, so I hired two part-time employees and finally was able to put effort into growing my business.

Many of my managerial skills came from Shauna. I knew from the beginning how important mentoring and coaching were and honed those skills during my year as a manager in Oklahoma City. I continued to improve them during the years after my bosses bought the wildlife control company and let me run that division. I'd briefly forgotten how well I could manage, mentor, and coach others as I lost myself in the work and minutiae of running my own business. Once I put those skills back into play and hired others, my business took off.

My mantra for hiring has always been *Attitude, mindset, and integrity will take the day.* It's easy to teach technical skills, but it may not be worth your time to coach someone with a closed mindset or negative attitude. If they don't have integrity, you don't even want them on your property.

The first part-time technician I hired and trained, my cousin Aaron, removed a lot of pressure from my time. Immediately I started working smarter and more efficiently, making the most of the time he gave me. Next, I hired a part-time office administrator, Lena's friend Maria, and she started digging into the months of paperwork I'd piled up on my desk. I was mortified when she found unmailed invoices from the previous year. They generated enough income to pay her wages for months. I admitted that my paperwork skills weren't up to par, and I was more than happy to delegate that work to someone who was much better at it.

Aaron and Maria were the genesis of my business growing bigger and better. As soon as they joined me and I focused on building, not just doing the work myself, we began expanding. Before long, Aaron quit his job and became my full-time lead technician, and Maria became my full-time office manager. From there we grew fast, adding new employees and equipment, and outgrowing offices, and I ensured we *all* made good money while my business made substantial profits. Our plans include further expansion into new locations and buying other businesses. Bats to Rats LLC is a multi-million-dollar business, something I didn't imagine in 2015.

What makes me proud is not just our financial success, but the quality of our teamwork. I make a point of empowering our employees, encouraging them to grow individually and within their teams. As soon as they're thoroughly trained, I let them know I trust them to run the company without looking over their shoulders or second-guessing them. Invariably, they live up to my expectations.

My family doesn't hesitate now to take vacations almost monthly. Each boy gets a separate trip to a place of their choice on their birthday, and Lena and I are making up for years of not traveling. I have complete confidence in my team's ability to keep the ship sailing on course when I'm not around to steer it myself.

> "Attitude, mindset, and integrity will take the day."

As I'm writing this chapter, I have a new *Men's Health* magazine sitting on the corner of my desk. An article in the issue documents the transformational health journey I began in 2021 when Franklin, my youngest son, described me to his preschool class as his "400-pound beer-chugging dad."

At that point I weighed about 70 pounds less than he gave me credit for, but let's not split hairs. Franklin didn't lie. I was big, fat, and drank more than my share of beer. It was good beer, mind you— the very best craft beer—but it added nothing to my life but calories. The shock of hearing Franklin's description of me made it clear I needed to make changes again, and this time they'd better stick.

I've been a big guy all my life. At six-three, I'm broad-shouldered and muscular after years of football and an adult life filled with active, outdoor work; my body can carry quite a bit of extra weight without it being too obvious. But just because I can camouflage it doesn't mean I've not been obese most of my adult years. From a low of about 225 pounds when I was 21, I'd gained steadily throughout my twenties. I was still healthy, but my weight was headed in the wrong direction.

Have you heard of the gas station diet? Service people who are out in their trucks driving from house to house—pest-control technicians like me, delivery people, even construction crews on the move—stop for fast food at those big, multi-pump service stations. They're fast in, fast out, offering a wide variety of super-high-fat/high-salt fast-food choices (all terrible for you), huge soft drinks, and crunchy snacks. It's cheap food in every sense of the word and meant to be eaten fast and anything but mindfully in your vehicle. And that's what I ate for years. Lots of it.

At age 28, just a year after starting my business, I was tipping the scales at 300 pounds. I met a self-described holistic health coach, and she sold me a variety of powdered vegetable and fruit pills to help me lose weight and become healthier. I became a vegetarian and then a vegan for a while, and over a year I lost 75 pounds. The "coach" just sold me the pills and didn't encourage me to add protein to my diet or work out, so I lost much of my muscle as well as fat. At the end of the year, I may have been thinner, but I was also flabby and weak, not healthy at all. The diet wasn't sustainable.

The next stage in my health trip was working out, which I should have done in the first place but hadn't since I'd been on the football squad in high school. This phase didn't last long because I was stealing time from my family, especially Lena. I'm the kind of person who dives full bore into everything, and working out was no exception. I wouldn't lift weights for 45 minutes or an hour; no, I spent hours every evening on my workout program after the kids were in bed. That, too, wasn't sustainable. I have a wonderful partnership with my wife, and Lena and I need time together. My workout stole what time was available for us.

Rather than cutting back, I foolishly quit working out altogether and dove into the effervescent world of high-end craft beers. I hadn't crossed the line into alcoholism, but I was afloat in beer, finding and drinking the best, rarest, and most exotic brews almost every day. It didn't take me long to gain back everything I'd lost plus another thirty pounds.

This was my situation when Franklin described me as his 400-pound, beer-chugging dad and gave me a wake-up call. It was time for me to show all three of my boys a dad they could look up to, someone who could keep up with them, have a healthy body, and take care of it. As their role model, I was setting a horrible example. As a husband, I wasn't giving Lena a promise that I'd be around for our retirement. I was letting everyone down, including my employees.

> Everyone needs a lighthouse.

At this point, I was in my mid-thirties and I knew I was running out of time. Middle age was right around the corner, and I wanted to enter it as healthy as I could make myself. Not just thinner, but healthy inside and out. It was time to make major adjustments to my mindset.

I started to eat with good nutrition as my mindful goal, weighing my portions, drinking lots of water, keeping track of protein and carbs. I began to walk every day; my new desk has a built-in treadmill, and my Zoom calls are notable because my head's bobbing rhythmically as I stride along, a guaranteed 10-15,000 steps every day. I began resistance training, adding weights, working out several days a week, not daily, and not for hours at a time. My goal is to master moderation, not the usual modus operandi for my all-in personality.

The *Men's Health* article goes into more detail on my program and includes several before-and-after sets of pictures. I'm now 240 pounds of muscle and bone with not much body fat, and I'm healthier than I've ever been. I'm proud of this portion of my personal transformation and the example I've set. We all need a "why," and mine is my family. My doctor, whom I now see regularly, says I've added more than a decade to the end of my life. Now my wellness journey has two lanes:

Every day I do my best to take care of myself, and I practice gratitude. I know I'll have a good day when I do them both.

A couple of years ago, I finally attended the National Wildlife Control Operators Association Expo and realized I too had the experience and ideas to offer my fellow business owners. Since then, I've been speaking at expos and conferences, and to my own surprise I enjoy it. I'm considered an authority on the wildlife control business, and my health and personal development journeys are fair game as much as my business journey.

If sharing what I learned can change others' lives or help them find their potential, I'm all in. One of my greatest joys is helping people succeed. I love showing people what's possible when they adjust their mindset, see their potential, and believe in their own greatness.

I am irked by the hypocrisy of coaches who don't live the lives they talk about, who've never done what they've preached, or who don't admit to their mistakes. We learn by our mistakes as well as our good choices, and I've made more than my share of both. People can be affected by the choices others make, and I want to inspire them to make their own good choices.

When I was only 18 years old and Shauna began to mentor me, I learned that everyone needs a lighthouse. I saw firsthand the difference one made in my life. Now it's my turn to be the beacon to help others navigate their journey and reach their goals. When someone's path is easier because of something I've shared, whether they're my team members, my audience, or they've read one of the books I've written, I'm more than gratified. I'm rewarded.

ABOUT DAINE PATTON

The owner of Bats to Rats Wildlife Control and Prevention, a company he founded in 2015, Daine has spent almost two decades working in the pest and wildlife industry. What began as a one-man operation has grown into a thriving business with a full-time team serving all of Nebraska and parts of Kansas, Missouri, and Iowa. In 2024, Bats to Rats was honored with the Better Business Bureau's Torch Award for Ethics—recognition of the company's commitment to integrity and high standards.

Daine's professional success is matched by a powerful personal transformation. Once a 330-pound man stuck in unhealthy patterns, he committed to changing his life. Over the past four years, he has lost 116 pounds, quit drinking alcohol, and embraced a mindset built on growth, discipline, and consistency. His focus on health, family, gratitude, and business has reshaped every part of his life.

Married to his wife Lena since 2011, Daine is a devoted husband and father to three boys—Charles, Harvey, and Franklin. He believes in leading by example and living a life aligned with the values he hopes to pass on to his children.

Whether building his business or becoming the best version of himself, Daine lives with purpose. He is passionate about helping others break free from excuses and live a life they're proud of.

 Batstorats.com

 Instagram: @dainepatton

Facebook: @dainepatton

Step Into The Arena

LT. COL. JEFF TIEGS,
U.S. ARMY SPECIAL FORCES (RET.)

President Theodore Roosevelt's "Man in the Arena" speech is one of the most quoted of all time, even after 115 years, and it's a favorite of mine. To paraphrase the part that always speaks to me: *There is a hero inside each of us, waiting to rise. Step into the arena. Stand your ground. Become that hero.*

Victims of sex trafficking deserve our undivided attention and our help. They deserve heroes who step into the arena and make things right.

The victims didn't have my attention or my help for the 25 years I was in U.S. Army Special Forces. Instead, I was focused on tracking down al-Qaeda, ISIS, ruthless dictators who overstepped their boundaries, and other enemies of the United States. Yes, I saw horrific sexual abuse. But I dismissed it as a foreign problem, and not one I was tasked to address.

Manuel Noriega, the president/dictator of Panama, turned buildings he owned into vast brothels filled with sex slaves, both young girls and boys. I was a young enlisted man when we overthrew his government, and I can still describe the horror of those places. I'll never forget my first exposure to sex trafficking at a commercial scale.

Al-Qaeda would kidnap entire villages and for the men, it was *convert or die*. They'd divide up or sell off the women and girls to be used as sex slaves in whatever manner the buyer wanted. I knew what was happening, but rescuing these girls was not the priority mission.

I felt the call to take on the commercial sex trafficking scourge in 2011 when I was studying at the Naval War College in Rhode Island. I had the first glimmer of a vision for Skull Games Solutions (SGS), but I couldn't do much more than start outlining plans for what is now my full-time mission—and pray to God for guidance. When I left the Army four years later and could make my own choices, God laid this job on me. I've been a commando my entire adult life, and now I'm able to choose my own targets: online commercial sex traffickers and the predators who pay to abuse the victims.

I founded SGS, a fast-growing 501 (c) (3) nonprofit that hunts sexual predators, and I knew immediately that I would be doing this for the rest of my life. I'm already training my replacement and will make sure others can carry on when I can't. Of course, I'll always be involved as long as I'm alive.

Working in counterterrorism taught me most of the techniques I need in my "retirement" job. I still hunt predators. They're just as evil, and I'm just as determined to put them away. The work is important, as intense as my military missions, and just as satisfying. I did not have hope that we would win the wars in Afghanistan and Iraq. And I don't expect to win a war against sex traffickers, but I will fight it. I'm a fighter, and my new opponents are American pimps and sex predators.

Though males and females of all ages are also being trafficked, most of the survivors we identify and rescue are young women. Currently, we work exclusively in the United States. We've reached the point where we're ready to scale up, and in the not-too-distant future, SGS will go global.

Skull Games Solutions gets its name from a notorious pimp, Iceberg Slim. He said, accurately and memorably, ***Pimping ain't a sex game, it's a skull game.***

Traffickers are excellent at getting complete control inside their victims' heads. Understand, the victims are not prostitutes or criminals. They're rape victims, raped as often as someone is willing to pay for them, seven days a week, until they're no longer profitable money-makers. I repeat, they are *victims* and never responsible for the crimes attached to them. It's part of the game. Traffickers compel their victims to commit crimes, deliberately destroying any remaining sense of safety beyond the trafficker's control. The predators who control them, profit from them, and sell them are wholly responsible, and they're our primary targets.

Those who pay to rape and abuse create the demand and share the responsibility. They are predators and deserve whatever the law throws at them. They're rapists, often *child* rapists, and we supply the information police need so they can be identified and interdicted too.

Until all too recently, law enforcement would arrest the victims and charge them with the crime of prostitution. While they arrested the pimps if they could identify them, often they'd let the predatory men who abused the victims go free. Thank God that has mostly changed, though not all jurisdictions have updated their approach.

We have an unyielding policy: SGS won't work with law enforcement organizations that still arrest victims of sex trafficking. We also work only with those organizations that have brought us in for training.

Our mantra is *identify, interdict,* and *empower.* We use most of the same open source intelligence techniques as we did when we were going after al-Qaeda, and the Special Forces motto, *Free the Oppressed,* applies equally well to the work we do at Skull Games. We're still commandos, but our work is all intelligence and training; we don't arrest or punish the predator ourselves.

What's particularly insidious about sexual trafficking in the United States is that the cute, young, all-American girl or boy next door is the most valuable. The pimp's most prized victim isn't the drug addict or beat-up runaway you might imagine. The money-makers they look for are cute, healthy kids, still of school age, targeted by "boyfriends" who begin to groom, control, and isolate them, the younger the better.

Often the trafficker is an older man, an experienced predator, but he can also be a teenager with criminal instincts. The groomer separates their victims from whatever it is that completes or fulfills them, whatever brings them joy, whether it's music, art, a horse, athletics, or their family. The next steps are easier: He systematically takes away their self-worth, their innocence, their youth, and even their health, both mental and physical.

Rather than sell drugs or weapons, certain criminals find it less risky to sell humans to perverts who know exactly what they're getting. They're playing the odds because only one percent of trafficking criminals are ever prosecuted. We want to change these odds and make trafficking far less attractive to risk-averse criminals. I believe that once 12-15 percent of them are caught and prosecuted, the tide will turn. If enough traffickers are caught and prosecuted, they'll start switching their efforts to something else.

Most traffickers sell four to five women online simultaneously. They offer you a checklist—what services you want, for how long—and you just place your order.

The girls and women we focus on are marketed and sold as "escorts," which makes them sound as though they're a wannabe Julia Roberts right out of *Pretty Woman.* They're not standing on a street corner, wearing revealing clothes. Their online photos highlight their youth, their wholesomeness, and imply they're happy to participate in your wildest fantasies.

As long as you have a phone, internet access, and money, it's as easy to go to an "escort" site and arrange for a young body to be delivered to your door as it is to order a pepperoni pizza via DoorDash. Understand, the service is in every neighborhood, even good ones, even *your* neighborhood, and not just the shady parts of town.

We focus on finding minors because no person who has not attained age 18 can engage in a sex act for profit. That is trafficking. That is the law. If the victim is 18 or older, the federal code for commercial sex trafficking requires proof that the pimp used "force, threats of force, fraud, or coercion." Those four things, especially coercion, can be *very* hard to prove.

When women grow older and are still being trafficked, their mortality rate climbs steeply. Many of them are lost to suicide or drug overdoses and physical or mental illness. Being trafficked does not lead to a long life or long-term career.

The word "trafficked" has been in the news so much lately that it's in danger of losing its impact. Let's put it in brutal perspective: Imagine your teenage daughter or sister being raped a dozen times a day, day after day, by all types of perverts who are looking for a child on whom they can act out their worst sexual fantasies.

Trafficking is exactly that evil, and the word should never be whitewashed or downplayed.

My years as a Special Forces officer has guided me in my post-Army life. I had run many teams of various sizes, but only within the discipline of the service. I knew I needed to add specific non-military training before I could effectively run a civilian organization. One of my first moves was to supplement the master's degree in International Relations and Strategic Studies I'd earned at the Naval War College, so I enrolled in an executive business course at Stanford University. What I learned from that intense program helped me kickstart Skull

Games Solutions and design a better organization from the ground up. Fortunately, my leadership style is strongly based on mentoring, so I didn't have to re-learn leadership as well as organizational concepts.

When I launched SGS, I knew this project would keep me busy for the rest of my life. I invited other veterans to share my vision, knowing I needed a hundred different skill sets; each of the people on my team has dozens. My core, full-time team of six is equally divided by gender, though a majority of the women are in supervisory positions. My part-time team of a dozen veterans who serve as consultants is also equally divided between women and men.

Our team is supplemented by 500 volunteer members who are vetted and trained through a structured process, including background checks and quarterly training events around the country. They've all passed our certified open-source intelligence (OSINT) training program and serve as hunters, including survivor hunters who have survived trafficking themselves. The survivors educate us and our law enforcement contacts every day.

After a decade of hard work, Skull Games is becoming a *ten-year overnight success*, a term I learned at Stanford and can now apply without irony to my own nonprofit. We're recognized as the top counter-sex-trafficking task force in the United States and can legitimately announce that we're law enforcement's preferred partner. They now reach out to us and ask for help.

For our first eight years, we supported other organizations, and in 2023, we went out on our own, while still limiting ourselves to working in the United States. We modeled our interaction with different jurisdictions on Special Forces, using the same techniques that gave us our most effective inroads into al-Qaeda and ISIS. In Iraq and Afghanistan, a small group of us worked at the local level with their village elders and local law enforcement. Our trafficking work uses the same formula: We don't do arrests or help with prosecution, what you'd define as law enforcement work. We supply the intelligence work.

We work primarily with local law enforcement agencies because working with federal agencies requires a tremendous amount of dancing through bureaucratic hoops. Also, federal officers focus more often on child sexual abuse materials, including pornography, rather than trafficking.

The training we supply is a key reason we've been accepted so thoroughly by local police and deputies. Before we collaborate with the officers in any new jurisdiction, we go on-site for a three-day training session, working closely with the personnel who will be implementing the intelligence we supply. We spend the first day and a half training the officers, and they learn how we support them with analytical and operational support.

During the second half of day two, we give them the intelligence packets we've prepared. Using OSINT, we've identified local traffickers, predators, and victims. On day three, law enforcement officers interdict (arrest) the predators, and the victims are turned over to a variety of victim support services for housing, medical care, and psychological support.

Fortunately, social services in most jurisdictions have evolved enough to understand and meet the victims' need for extended support. Enough trafficking victims have told their stories on public stages that the stigma and shame victims feel is dissipating. People realize the victims need support and healing, not punishment, and advocates and social services are available. Still, survivors' full recovery, what we call "restoration," can take years, if it ever happens.

Though part of our mission is to empower the survivors, we don't work with them right after their rescue but wait until they're ready. Then, we offer weekend retreats where they learn Brazilian jiu-jitsu, how to handle and feel comfortable with weapons, and to shoot accurately. It's been scientifically proven these activities help rewire their brains, helping them heal faster and more completely.

The only boundaries SGS has are financial, as is the case with most nonprofits. To help raise our profile and generate donations, I've signed with a speaker's bureau and am traveling around the country, talking to a variety of civic and business organizations, ranging from Rotary Clubs to groups of venture capitalists.

When I joined the Army the first time, I was a naïve 17-year-old from Pewaukee, a small town in Wisconsin, hungry for adventure and challenge. For twelve years, I attended a Lutheran parochial school where I volunteered for student government, ran track, and wrestled. I was ready for a seismic shift in my life.

I didn't think college was in my future and the Army seemed like a natural option, though my family didn't have a long history of military service and I wasn't sure what I'd face. An uncle had gone to Vietnam, but for some reason we didn't talk about his experience. Once I enlisted, I quickly learned that the men I lived and worked among were committed to a code of service I'd never imagined.

The men who trained me and those with whom I worked welcomed hardship. They taught me excellence was not an end result but a pursuit, a discipline that proved itself in the smallest details. Endurance and adaptability are valued more than sheer strength. I knew I had finally found my niche.

Though I never set out to be a leader, I became one while I was still 17 years old. Since then, leadership has been my constant responsibility, one I've never been able or willing to ignore.

Joining Special Forces became my goal as soon as I learned more about the elite groups in the Army. There are several, but the most famous are the Green Berets and Delta Force. They both focus on counterterrorism and unconventional warfare, and are made up of seasoned veterans, mostly in their thirties. The Rangers are another elite group, made up of younger men, a relatively small light infantry group that raids and does reconnaissance in more conventional ways.

The second I was eligible, I completed Jump School, determined to become a Ranger. After Jump School, I knew I was on the list to try out, but when names were called for us to get on the bus, mine wasn't one of them. I ran to find the keeper of the lists, a mysterious and obnoxious man who played mind games with me before promising he'd call in my name to the guardian of the gate at the Ranger Assessment and Selection Program (RASP). Jules, my girlfriend (now wife), drove me to where the Ranger candidates were already getting hazed, and my name had suddenly reappeared on the list. I was in.

> " I've been pursuing justice all my life. "

I made it through training and earned my black beret (now the Ranger beret is tan). To me, the next step was Delta Force, but my eyesight wasn't perfect and I was disqualified from trying out. You might think the super elite units are a big, beefy young man's game, but it's no game, and it's not for the very young. Those who do qualify are usually ten years older than most Rangers—wiry, smart, strong guys at the peak of their mental and physical powers, with a lot of miles under their boots. Delta Force operators are disciplined, high-performing, mature, and have incredible endurance. They're all sergeants or officers with years of exceptional service. Adaptability is one of their main strengths because it's key to survival in small-unit warfare.

I extended my Army service for a year so I could attend sniper school and go through scuba training. During my enlistment, I earned my sergeant stripes and spent five years meeting goals and leading others. The Rangers had already taught me to see the world in a broader way than the myopic view I had when I joined. By the time I was discharged, I had the confidence to know I was suited for college after all. I was ready to make the most of the GI Bill and earn a degree.

In high school, I hadn't thought I was fast enough in track or good enough in wrestling to compete at the college level, which I thought of as the big leagues. I soon found out that I was certainly fast enough. The Army had added layers of endurance to my original speed, and I was competitive in NCAA Division One track and cross country. Running steadied me throughout college and kept me anchored in everyday life.

After two years at University of North Carolina at Wilmington, I was ready to experience something new. I knew I wanted to live in the mountains, so Jules and I moved to Bozeman, Montana, and I transferred to Montana State, where I majored in psychology. The university sponsored a Reserve Officers' Training Corps program (ROTC), and I noticed the instructors seemed a little short-handed. Idly, I thought that perhaps I could volunteer with some of the cadet training, and I showed up wearing a beard, shaggy and not looking very spit-shined, offering, "Can I help?" I was enrolled as a ROTC cadet before I could say *That's not what I meant!*

When I graduated with my degree in psychology, I also was commissioned back into the Army, this time wearing a gold second lieutenant's bar on my chest. I attended Infantry Officer Basic Course, where once I qualified, I was slotted back into the Rangers.

Before being qualified to try out for Delta Force, I needed to have a successful command as a captain. I had the honor of this command with the 10th Special Forces Group, where I deployed to combat numerous times, honing my warrior skills. Eye surgery had improved so much over the past few years that I'd decided to risk the laser option, and after the surgery my eyesight met the Delta Force standards.

After joining the ranks of Delta Force and returning to combat numerous times, it was time to return to my family.

The Code of Laws of the United States of America (Code) is a list of all laws enacted by Congress, both civil and criminal. Section 1591 of the Code deals with commercial sex trafficking, and it's broken down into degrees of criminal liability depending on the victim's age: children under 14, teenagers 14-17 who are trafficked by any means, and 18 and over who are trafficked via force, fraud, or coercion, as I touched on earlier. The penalties vary, but they're severe—up to life in prison under certain circumstances.

Section 1591 is also the name of a documentary on child sex trafficking that's being released in 2026. Skull Games is listed as an executive producer, and I'm the protagonist. We interviewed an 18-year-old trafficking survivor who still looked 13, despite what she had endured. She was never tattooed because her pimp wanted to keep her looking innocent and almost pre-pubescent.

When she told her story, I related to her trauma, and I think most soldiers who've experienced combat would, too. She endured the years of unbearable horrors by compartmentalizing her trauma, as all soldiers need to do with their battle experiences in order to cope. On the outside, we couldn't be more different. On the inside, our techniques for successfully dealing with and surviving our trauma is very similar.

I've studied trafficking survivors and sat down with them to more fully understand what they go through, how they survive, and how to help them. The ones who survive are damaged, but they're tough. They never had the support and training we soldiers did, and most importantly, they never volunteered for what happened to them. You could make the case for them being even tougher than many battle-hardened military survivors.

From the beginning of my service career, I've had more stability in my personal life than many other soldiers enjoyed. Faith had been woven into the fabric of my childhood, both from my Lutheran parochial school and my parents. What I believed and how I originally saw the world were shaped by faith.

I was young when I learned the meaning of *hesed*, a Hebrew word with rich meaning, impossible to translate to just one or even several English words: loyal love, steadfast and unshakable, mercy, grace, faithfulness, and commitment. Hesed also recognizes that the world is not as it's meant to be and is instead broken. Hesed goes beyond an emotion, and living with hesed means working on behalf of someone in need. Living with hesed also means accepting the responsibility to mend what can be mended; it's the pursuit of justice and compassion while we still have our breath. I've been pursuing justice and doing my best to be compassionate all my life.

My parents were blue-collar folks who believed that work was a duty and it brought us dignity. Dad's work was trimming trees along power lines, and it was brutal. In the summer he'd come home soaked from hours of climbing poles and cutting branches. Sweat would pour from his boots when we kids pulled them off.

In the winter, Dad would come home with icicles hanging from his beard, his clothes stiff and frozen to his body. He'd head straight for the basement, sit in front of the word-burning stove, and thaw out in silence. Even as a child I couldn't understand how the human body could endure what his did, much why a man would voluntarily do it.

Years later, I realized I'd followed in his footsteps; I'd become one of those men.

I met Julianne (or "Jules" as I referred to her previously) when we were fifteen years old and worked together at a local restaurant. We married at 19 and we waited until I graduated from college before we started our family. As we grew up together away from our families, Jules grounded me during all of my training, assignments, and deployments.

Becoming a father was the most pivotal moment of my life; *everything* shifted. I immediately felt a profound responsibility and realized the full extent of what I had to live for. Seeing first Aaron's birth and then Jonah's three years later filled me with awe, both at the miracle of new life and for the woman who was the mother of our children.

At first, I was sure fatherhood would temper my hunger for risk and adventure, but the opposite happened. My responsibilities only sharpened my drive. I felt the need to show my sons what it means to me to be a man: to be strong, capable, a protector, and someone who savors every moment of adventure in life.

Jules took on the burden of breaking the news of my leaving for deployment to the boys after the fact, comforting them so I wouldn't have to. I'd wait until Aaron and Jonah were tucked into bed, and I'd leave the house quietly, no goodbyes, and most importantly to me, no tears. It was easier for me to start my deployment without guilt and drama, and I was convinced that ritual was easier for them, especially after saying goodbye to them just once. Their reaction to seeing me leave had broken my heart and I knew theirs were broken as well.

> " I live as though my life is borrowed time "

Jules always wiped their tears, reassured them, and carried her own fear in silence, shouldering it all so I could leave for war unencumbered by guilt. It was hard on her, and I think she too was a casualty of war though she was never in combat. I'm doing my best now to make up for the burden I placed on her for all those years.

Whenever I was in combat, I made a bargain with God: I told Him I'd fight with everything in me, I'd be willing to sacrifice pieces of my body, but I asked in return for Him to keep me alive so I could return to my sons. I wanted to be fully present and be a full-time father. God kept His end of the deal. I came home in one piece, retired, and now my boys are not just my sons but my best friends.

The bargain feels complete, and I am at peace. I know He could take me at any time and I would understand. I live as though my life is borrowed time; it's given back to me, but it's also meant to be used well by helping others.

Our family moved to Bend, Oregon when I retired; I was determined we'd spend the time we had together in the mountains. Though I was busy starting up SGS, I made time to write, which I learned to love while I was in college.

My first published book was Where Have All the Heroes Gone? A Pilgrimage Through the Bible, the Battlefield and Back Home Again. While I was serving on deployments, I always relied on Bible stories to keep me centered and inspired. In my book, I retell some of those stories through the lens of a warrior, weaving in my own experiences, offering my readers a new perspective.

My next book will be the first in a series exploring how *words shape worlds*, focusing first on Eden, then Sinai, Galilee, and finally Jerusalem; it's still in the works and should be published within the next year. As I hope you can clearly see, my faith underlies all I strive for. Writing is no exception.

As I settle into this new season of my life, I realize I've left one battlefield behind for another. Though the rules of engagement have changed, I know I still see a hero inside each of us, waiting to rise.

Don't hesitate.

Step into the arena. Stand your ground. Become that hero.

ABOUT JEFF TIEGS

As a Special Forces operator, Jeff spent more than 25 years leading teams of our country's most elite soldiers, hunting terrorists and our enemies around the world. Since retiring in 2015, he's devoted his life to hunting sex traffickers. His battlefield and targets have changed, but his mission to combat evil has not.

Ten years ago, Jeff founded Skull Games Solutions (SGS), a 501(c)(3) nonprofit organization, and recruited veterans who use their years of open source intelligence experience to locate traffickers and their victims online. Five hundred trained volunteers support Jeff's core staff of men, women, and survivors. SGS experts train and support local law enforcement agencies which arrest both the traffickers and the predators who pay for the victims.

Trafficking survivors are introduced to victim services for help in recovering from their trauma. When the survivors are ready, they're invited to attend SGS retreats where they're taught weapons skills and Brazilian jiu-jitsu as part of their recovery, or "restoration" as Jeff calls the process.

Looking for adventure, Jeff joined the Army at age 17. After five years, he left the service to attend college, graduating with a degree in psychology and a commission as an Army second lieutenant. The Army later sent him to the Naval War College in Rhode Island for a master's degree in international relations and strategic studies.

Section 1591, a documentary scheduled to be released in 2026, stars Jeff and his team. Jeff has published ***Where Have All the Heroes Gone?***, in which he retells favorite Bible stories through the lens of a warrior. His upcoming book is the first in a series that traces how words throughout the Bible do more than awaken life; they summon it, steady it, direct it, and ultimately fulfill it. He, his wife, Jules, and their two sons live in Bend, Oregon.

Skull Games Solutions

https://skullgames.org

LinkedIn: Skull Games

X: @SkullGames.io

Facebook: Skull Games Task Force

Instagram: @skullgamessolutions

Jeff Tiegs

Website: jefftiegsbooks.com

LinkedIn: Jeff Tiegs

Facebook: Jeff Tiegs

Instagram: @jefftiegs

Bloom Where You're Planted

COLONEL TAMMY S. HINSKTON, USAF, (RETIRED)

"**Y**ou're never going to be an officer! You'll never make it through this program!" my training instructor screamed at me in front of my fellow officer candidates. It was a horrific first day in the program, and I called my dad that evening, trying to hide my tears from the other cadets.

"I want to give up and come home," I said when I reached him.

My dad, an Air Force lieutenant colonel who'd survived field training decades before, broke through my internal pity party. I listened intently to his pep talk as he reminded me I'm a strong, independent, educated woman who grew up in the military and could succeed in anything I set my mind to.

He also reminded me to remember why I was there and that it wasn't supposed to be easy.

"Take it one hour, one meal, and then one day at a time, and do your best, always," Dad said.

I was ready to change the world when I got off the phone.

My identity has been in the military since my birth at an Air Force Base. I was raised believing everybody knew how to iron their clothes, make beds with hospital corners, and always respect authority. My parents taught me work ethic, how to recover from mistakes, and how *not* to quit. I owe much of my personal and professional success to the lessons they instilled in me as a child.

When I was young, I planned to marry someone in the military and be the ideal officer's wife, just like my mom. I realized early enough that I'd never survive in that role, but I was well into my twenties before I knew I was much more suited to being an officer myself.

We had the typically peripatetic Air Force life—Germany, England, Virginia, Ohio, New Mexico, and back to Germany. In fact, I started kindergarten and finished high school at Ramstein AB, which serves as headquarters for the Air Force in Europe and Africa and the NATO Allied Air Command.

My childhood went smoothly, and I excelled at art, math, and volleyball. But after high school, I couldn't figure out my future. I dropped out of the University of New Mexico during my sophomore year, returned to Ramstein, where my parents remained posted, and worked in catering at the officers' club. It was a harbinger of my future Air Force career, though I never had to come home smelling like food when I was running base clubs and services as an officer.

When my younger sister went off to college at Colorado State University, our father's alma mater, I gave college another try and joined her. I still was drifting, career-wise; my major changed from mathematics (too hard), architecture (too many years to get a degree), and interior design (I couldn't abide the free spirits of my fellow design students), to Human Development and Family Studies, with the intent of getting certified as a teacher. I finally interned and taught living, breathing students during my senior year. I soon realized teaching was not the path for me either!

In the middle of my career crisis, I aged out of the military-dependent identification card or ID program, which took away my access to military bases and the military identity I'd known all my life.

The solution finally hit me, and I signed up for Officer Training School (OTS). Shortly after graduating from college, I received my acceptance. Unfortunately, I had to postpone attending for months after I was concussed during a softball game. The day finally arrived, one I will never forget: November 27, the start of an incredible Air Force career.

After my first-day jitters and my dad's pep talk, I did exceptionally well at OTS and graduated in the top four of my class as Officer Trainee Colonel Hinskton, Mission Support Group Commander. I held on to those eagles as motivation to someday outrank my dad, who'd retired as a lieutenant Colonel. He and my fiancé, EJ, participated in my 1996 commissioning ceremony. My dad shaved his beard, wore his dress uniform, swore me in, and received my first salute. EJ, a technical sergeant in the Colorado Air National Guard, gave me my first salute from an enlisted man, and I gave him the traditional silver dollar in return.

While my career goals included eventually becoming a full colonel and outranking my dad, my leadership style was never focused on self-promotion. My drive to succeed was tempered by my empathy, and I always took care of those I commanded. As I was tested by each new assignment and challenge, my passion to serve my enlisted airmen, officers, and civilian employees never wavered, and I added new leadership and management tools at every posting.

I had the privilege of traveling the world with my family and continuing my education. I was exposed to both excellent and bad leaders, learning from both to become the leader who would wear those coveted eagles, accomplish missions, and impact lives along the way. I learned the valuable tools to lead people with excellence from the shoulders of giants. I have always valued integrity and honor.

EJ and I married four days before I reported to my first posting. I took his last name, perhaps the only traditional part of our marriage. He quit his weekday job and weekend warrior position in the Air National Guard to follow me to my new assignment. He also gave me three bonus babies when we married—not exactly babies, but his two beautiful girls, Jaime and Brandy, and a teenage son, Jeremy. Our children spent holidays and summers with us as they grew up, and we are a close family.

The South was a shock to me. EJ, my husband, is Black, and we were not prepared for overt racism, as we realized when he was profiled by a security guard at my OTS graduation in Alabama. It turned out that Arkansas' racism was just about as loud and proud as it was in the deep South. I met a realtor when I was house-hunting off-base on my own. The realtor reassured me, a blonde officer, "This is a safe neighborhood and a great place to live because there are only two Black families."

"We're *done* looking," I snapped, and quickly returned to my car. Later, I discovered I could have reported her, and she would have lost the right to work with military families. I wish I'd known.

Since EJ paid child support, and I was paying off student loans, we weren't in a position to live solely on my second lieutenant's salary. While he waited for a full-time Air National Guard position to open up, he took whatever work he could find, which turned out to be dragging ball fields. Unfortunately, he was a big-city guy from Denver who didn't like anything resembling outdoor wildlife. He hated the bugs, dust, and humidity and despised coming home dirty every night. He stuck it out and finally landed a full-time position on base as a Technical Sergeant. Unfortunately he had to find a new job every time we relocated over the course of my career.

As a young officer, I worked hard to develop my leadership skills and take care of my people. I started as a food service officer, afraid I would fail because I wasn't a great cook. My dad reminded me I was there to lead and not to cook, a lucky thing for everyone who ate at the dining hall. I learned to ask many questions and also to trust but verify. I started to hit my stride when I standardized operations across three facilities. I made sure I knew fully what our needs and shortfalls were so that when a senior leader stopped by, I could give my elevator speech requesting funds. It worked; I landed $65,000 for facility maintenance and repairs; my boss was flabbergasted.

My parents had taught me to "bloom where you're planted" because you don't know who is watching or where this job will lead. That lesson has always influenced my career—no place more strongly than in Little Rock. Arkansas was the last place I wanted to go, but I worked hard, cared for my people, volunteered to repair homes after tornados hit the surrounding towns, and helped build houses with Habitat for Humanity. When the resource management position became unexpectedly vacant, I was selected to fill it and run the flight. I was a second lieutenant, filling the position of a GS-12, which is equivalent to a major. I was picked because I could lead, not because of my accounting skills.

> " My career was my responsibility. "

I bloomed, and most people on base knew me because of my accomplishments at such a junior grade. Because I had bloomed, I was selected as a full-time student for a coveted position to attend the University of Las Vegas, Nevada. I obtained my Master of Science in Hotel and Restaurant Administration, which set me up for a successful career in the Air Force.

Unfortunately, not everything at my first post was perfect. My bosses discovered my husband, the highly visible and popular DJ at the officers' club, was an enlisted member and tried to bring us up on bogus fraternization charges. The creation of fraternization rules was meant to keep the chain of command untainted, with no romantic relationship allowed between an officer and an enlisted service member in their command structure. In our case, we were in different chains of command with absolutely no overlap; we had dated for three years before I even thought of a career in the Air Force. EJ and I were extra careful about being seen together on base in uniform, though it was fun having him salute me in public!

My Commander changed close to the end of my time at Little Rock AFB. The new Commander treated me like dirt and accused me of things I hadn't done. However, he didn't realize I had a reputation as an outstanding officer with the wing commander. I went over his head and made a formal complaint about his toxic, discriminatory, and unprofessional behavior. The Commander was counseled for his behavior, and I was super happy to get orders and leave that toxic environment.

We wanted to have a child as soon as possible, but my first pregnancy ended with a heartbreaking miscarriage. Our daughter, Toni, finally arrived shortly after my promotion to First Lieutenant; it was one of the happiest moments in my life. She's now 26 with her first child, and I wish her the same happiness that she always brought EJ and me.

I left Little Rock with the well-grounded understanding that it was up to me to bloom where the Air Force planted me; my career and happiness were my responsibilities. I won multiple awards at Little Rock, but didn't make my boss write them. Instead, I wrote them and submitted them after trusted peers edited them. Bosses are busy. They are happy to submit awards when deserved, but writing award packages takes time. Taking the initiative to give them a starting point increases the chances of submission.

I've operated on two beliefs throughout my career: *(1) Do not leave your career in someone else's hands, and (2) bloom where you're planted.*

The Air Force values education, and this was just the first of 15 separate educational opportunities I was afforded during my service. I was promoted to captain while I was still in school, and after I received my master's degree I was assigned to Nellis AFB just north of Las Vegas. EJ earned a traditional billet with the Reno Air National Guard and became a resident DJ at Caesar's Palace. After the extreme humidity in Arkansas, we appreciated Nevada and its climate, and neither of us were ready to leave Las Vegas yet.

My first deployment was to Aviano AB, Italy, to run the contingency complex in 2001. Two weeks after my arrival, we watched the September 11 attacks on TV. It was an uncertain few hours while we figured out what was happening and took action to secure the contingency complex. Here, I learned I excelled as a leader in a high-stress, unpredictable, and often dangerous environment. I returned to my Combat Support Flight Commander position at Nellis AFB for only a few months when I was deployed again to an undisclosed location. For six months, a female captain and I lived in a large tent with eight men on the other side of a six-foot interior wall.

Deployments often created a leadership challenge for me, particularly in countries where men don't do business with women. When I negotiated contracts, I was always accompanied by my male contract specialist, to whom the local power broker spoke, though the contract specialist always reminded the local leader that I was the decision maker. I treated my opposites respectfully, understood their culture, and hoped they'd reciprocate someday. Just before I left, the decision-maker finally spoke directly to me; I took it as a diplomatic win.

Following my Nellis AFB assignment, I spent the next three years in planning at the Air Expeditionary Force Center at Langley AFB. EJ retired from the Guard to follow me to Virginia and supply full-time parenting to Toni during our transitions before looking for a job for himself. Soon after my promotion to Major, I was assigned for two years to RAF Mildenhall, England, as the Services Squadron Commander, overseeing a team of 456 military and civilian personnel. I was responsible for a $14.7 million budget and ran 29 businesses and activities across 71 facilities.

Mildenhall was where my leadership moved to the next level. I more actively mentored young enlisted members as they were adjusting to the military life, especially young women who were often struggling so far from family. I helped them gain self-confidence and learn their value.

While in England, I polished my diplomatic and advanced leadership skills, a valid prerequisite for my future work at the Pentagon. I usually watched my words closely, except in one staff meeting when my brain broke and I accidentally called the Wing Commander "honey" during a discussion of post-Thanksgiving football at the Officers' Club. I was mortified, but everyone else, especially the Wing Commander, found it hilarious. When I tried apologizing, he said, "Don't! It was the best time I ever had at a staff meeting my entire career." I didn't live down "honey" for weeks. I learned that as a leader, you can't take yourself too seriously; it's good to laugh at your mistakes.

A third deployment to the United Arab Emirates took six months from the middle of my Mildenhall assignment. I was shocked when my eight-year-old daughter asked me if I had ever deployed before; she didn't remember that I had missed her third and fourth birthdays. This time, I pre-purchased and wrapped gifts for all the holidays/events I'd be absent from and filled a jar with one piece of candy for every day I'd be gone so she'd have a visual reminder of when I'd be home. I read books on DVD so she could watch me read to her. It was essential to stay connected to my family while I was gone. Video chatting wasn't available yet, just email and two 15-minute phone calls a week.

From England, we spent a year at the Naval Command and Staff College, where I earned my second master's. Then, Washington, D.C., became our stable home for the next nine years. My first Pentagon posting was three years as a Protocol Officer in the Office of the Chairman of the Joint Chiefs of Staff, during which time I was promoted to Lieutenant Colonel.

Here, I learned humility. I had come from positions where I had a large amount of both power and responsibility, but in protocol, I represented the CJCS. No one in the office was allowed to send anything out unless it had been checked by someone else to ensure it was error-free. I never realized how many mistakes I made; my goal was to get my products through error-free. I learned to welcome others' input and corrections because they made me better.

I moved into Public Affairs for the Secretary of the Air Force as Chief of Integrated Plans and Strategy. After the first year, I won the Action Officer of the Year Award and spent the second year deployed.

From 2013-14, I deployed to shut down the Transit Center at Manas in the Kyrgyz Republic, which had been a transfer point since 2001 for soldiers headed to Operation Enduring Freedom in Afghanistan. When I left for my year away from my family, Toni was 14, and it was not the easiest time to have your mother deploy. She and I have always been close, and I called her "my mini-me." When I don't recall something that happened while she was in high school, Toni reminds me plaintively, "That's the year you *left* me."

Four months before we closed the Transit Center, the base store ran out of sanitary products for women, which was unacceptable. I made phone calls to get resupply, calling up to the highest levels, but the store's leadership didn't want to get stuck with excess supply since we were shutting down. I finally gave up, went to the base chaplain, and asked him to contact his chaplain friends back in the United States to send us sanitary supplies. The chaplains came through, and we received many large boxes of supplies; we set them out in the women's dorm to take as needed, completely free. About a month later, the store on base finally received sanitary products. I've always believed there's more than one way to skin a cat. If regular channels didn't value our women, I'd find someone who did.

When I returned to the Pentagon, I became Senior Military Advisor to the Deputy Assistant Secretary of Defense for Military Community and Family Policy. I was back working with military members and their families, which was my passion. While in this position, my ability to lead a diverse group of people grew along with my ability to bloom where I'm planted. I trusted God to send me where He wanted me to be since He's bigger than the Air Force, and it was my job to do my very best wherever that ended up being.

Two years later, she was temporarily appointed as the executive to the Assistant Secretary of Defense for Manpower and Reserve Affairs. After 24 hours working for the ASD, he claimed me as his Senior Air Executive Officer, which is where I ended up for the next two years. When promotions came up, he had one "Definitely Promote" to give, and he gave it to me based on my records, history of exceptional performance, and what he'd experienced daily with my leadership. Two men I was competing against for the promotion to colonel told the ASD he was wrong and that they should have received the DP instead of me. One said if he was at "base level," he'd be able to hang out at the bar with the decision-makers and would have gotten the DP. That is the reality of a male-dominated career field, men can hang out with higher ranking male leaders at the bar or on the golf course whereas a female would be looked down upon if she were to hang out with her male peers or bosses at the bar or on the golf course.

Before my promotion ceremony to colonel, my retired dad shaved his beard to read me the oath of office. After the oath was complete, he saluted me and called me ma'am as his voice cracked; there was not a dry eye in the auditorium. When he turned smartly to return to his seat, the soles of his old military shoes disintegrated in a cloud of powdered rubber. Everybody howled, including my family.

While I was in that position, we had monthly birthday celebrations. I was the only woman in the office and a senior officer; however, I was always responsible for cutting and passing the cake and cleaning up after the celebration. After pulling cake duty a few times, I told my co-workers that everyone would be assigned a month to cut, pass, and clean up after the monthly celebration. There was unanimous agreement; everyone understood the unfairness. They honestly hadn't realized they were doing it.

A couple of months later, a new U.S. President was elected, and the ASD was temporarily replaced by a career civil servant, an amazingly talented female leader. During the next monthly birthday celebration, she picked up the knife, cut the cake, and handed the plates to me so I could pass them around. All the men in the office did a masterful job hiding their snickers as I gave them the evil eye. While our acting ASD was a talented servant leader, she managed to undo all I had done to forge equality in our office and ensure women weren't tagged with traditional women's work.

> "Do not leave your career in someone else's hands."

I finally returned overseas to Ramstein AB; not much had changed since I graduated high school. I served as the Division Chief, Readiness and Integration, for USAFE-AFAFRICA. We were excited to be back and explore Europe together. Toni was able to join us during summer and winter breaks from Denver University.

After two years in Germany, I was assigned another one-year unaccompanied assignment. I served as the 65 Air Base Group Commander of the United States portion of Lajes Field, Azores, Portugal plus Morón Air Base, Spain, two separate installations with runways totaling 130 million square feet. I led 1,200 personnel (military and civilian–U.S., Portuguese, and Spanish), $54 billion in contracts, and 1,200 facilities.

The United States had leased our side of Lajes Field, a Portuguese Air Force base and commercial airport, for more than 80 years since the last half of World War II. The strategic location also led to many rescues, and thanks to its long runways and Atlantic location, it was an alternate landing site for our moon shuttles.

I received three rare honors there, which still give me great pride. The Portuguese Air Force awarded me their Commendation

Medal, which is rarely given to non-Portuguese military officers. My fellow Group Commanders engraved a C-130 cargo aircraft window and presented it to me. The award was a real surprise because only commanders who work on the flight line usually receive them.

My final and most meaningful experience was being promoted to Honorary Chief Master Sergeant. This promotion is rarely given to officers, and it was awarded to me in recognition of how I care for my enlisted troops. Ironically, EJ had given up promotion to Chief Master Sergeant to follow me to Virginia 18 years before. This award is as much his as mine, not just for that reason but because he was always my sounding board and gave me a different perspective. Without his unwavering support, I would not have been as successful as I was.

I had always believed in going to bat for my troops and earned recognition through awards and commendations. I made the most of my craft skills in the Azores, which didn't have the resources other duty posts had. I used my Cricut to make stencils and etch various glass items I could find at the local shops, creating awards and trophies in a pinch. The troops loved them.

For my final two years, I returned to the USAF Headquarters at the Pentagon serving as the Services Operations Division Chief, Manpower, Personnel and Services Directorate, responsible for Services Operations worldwide.

Prejudice against women is sometimes so subtle and ingrained that people have no idea they're doing it, even in this modern age. My birthday cake and sanitary supplies stories are two small examples, and here's another from my last posting just a few years ago.

We were deploying for a weeklong exercise, and as usual, I looked over the housing list I received from the logistics coordinator. I noticed I had been assigned a roommate, but none of the other O-6/Colonel directors had roommates. I called the Major who sent the list, and he said, "Since you're the only female O-6 and the room is big, you'll have an O-5 (lieutenant colonel) for your roommate."

I pointedly asked, "Do any of the male O-6 directors have roommates?" and he said no. I paused to give him a chance to say more, then suggested, "Perhaps I shouldn't have a roommate if none of the other O-6 directors have them." That time, he got my point. I called the O-5, an outstanding officer, and explained, "You won't be my roommate on this trip, not because of who you are, but because when you are the only female O-6, you should get equal treatment and your own room. The standards shouldn't be lowered because there aren't as many of us."

After 27 1/2 years of duty in the Air Force, I retired in northern Virginia. I've been thinking about my leadership style and how I finally mastered work-life balance. I also thought a lot about mentoring, which is now an active part of my life and business.

While some other strong people helped and guided me, I never had a mentor who collaborated with me throughout my career. Many people have given me an à la carte menu of advice and choice tidbits to absorb that have filled my leadership toolbox. At the captain level, I was mentored by several higher officers.

Chuck Milam, the former Acting Deputy Assistant Secretary of Defense for Military Community and Family Policy, helped me get in front of the right people, in the right place, and at the right time to make the difficult jump to full colonel. Although I was running massive programs for DoD, I wasn't physically visible to senior leaders, and this lack of visibility can make it hard to reach the ranks above lieutenant colonel without people like Mr. Milam on your side.

Col. Michael Stough was the 100 Air Refueling Wing Commander when he showed me what exceptional servant leadership looks like. He let leaders lead, and when I made short-sighted decisions, he didn't make me change my decision but instead talked me through it and helped me realize how I could improve my strategic vision and grow as a leader.

Col. J.P. Mickle, my Group Commander at the Transit Center at Manas, showed me how to lead, mentor, and grow a team that feels like a family. He allowed me to make my own decisions as a leader, bounce ideas off him, or discuss proposed ideas and acceptable outcomes. He taught me the value of one-on-one mentorship with your direct reports and reinforced the value of relationships.

While I didn't lead formal mentoring programs at my command, I organized lunches with people of all different grades and led informal discussions about current events and upcoming changes. I made sure I was always approachable, and it was easy to ask me questions. I answered them with courtesy, always. Each Commander who reported to me had a one-on-one with me every week. I taught crafting classes because they allowed me to talk informally with my Airmen. As a woman of faith, I led the women's ministry during my deployments and remote assignments; my faith has always been important to me and has sustained me. There were always programs for men but limited programs for women, so I saw a need and filled it.

After I retired from the Air Force at the end of 2023, I founded Sawdust to Sunflowers LLC, a leadership development, mentoring, and coaching consultancy. I bring every leadership skill I developed into play and help my clients develop their own.

Through guided discussion, I help businesswomen overcome stereotypes so they can effectively communicate and confidently lead in a male-dominated career. *Through my Level-Up Your Leadership in 90-Days* program, leaders learn to increase their leadership confidence, improve communication skills, and avoid costly mistakes that lead to turnover.

I hope to be remembered as the person who successfully reminds others they are not the sum of their mistakes; instead, they're a beautiful work in progress, created to learn and grow through life's ups and downs.

ABOUT COLONEL TAMMY S. HINSKTON

Born into a career Air Force family, Tammy didn't discover her calling to military service until just months before college graduation. She and her family spent the next 27-plus years traveling the globe, calling wherever the Air Force sent them home.

Her 18 assignments and four deployments include almost a dozen years at the Pentagon, where she worked with the Secretary of Defense, Chairman of the Joint Chiefs of Staff, and Secretary of the Air Force in various high-level positions. She earned 37 medals and awards for her service, including three Legion of Merit Medals and the Portuguese Air Commendation Medal. In 2021, she had the rare honor of a promotion to Honorary Chief Master Sergeant in recognition of her dedication to serving the enlisted corps.

Tammy's servant leadership style was effective whether she led people or managed a budget and facilities in the United States, Europe, the Middle East, or Central Asia. She vowed there would be no toxic leadership during her watch and encouraged open communications at every level.

After retiring from the Air Force in 2023, Tammy founded Sawdust to Sunflowers LLC, a leadership development, coaching, and mentoring company. She had worked tirelessly to overcome roadblocks and stereotypes in the Air Force, both to thrive as a leader and to be a trail blazer for the women who followed her. Her experiences allowed her to design a coaching program to help businesswomen overcome stereotypes so they can effectively communicate and confidently lead in a male-dominated workplaces.

In 2025 she co-authored **On the Shoulders of Giants, Top-Producers Featuring Colonel Tammy S. Hinskton**, in which she shares her experiences in life and in leadership. This is her second title. Tammy and her husband, EJ, live in Northern Virginia.

Awaken the Greatness Within You

BRENDA PETRILLO

I have never been one to play small.

Not in how I love. Not in how I rise. Not in how I fight to reclaim my life.

Every countless challenge I've faced has offered me a binary choice: Stay in the familiar, silent, stuck, small, or take the hard right turn that will bring clarity, courage, and change. I refuse to let fear chain me to a life that isn't mine. You must stop waiting for someone to save you and save yourself.

I am not a tidy success story, but women don't need more perfection; we need more permission to rise messily, late, and loudly. My willingness to be transparent about my arduous journey gives me strength and is what I share with my co-authors. I'm not afraid to share the good and the bad because there is strength in vulnerability.

I have had days when I've built businesses and buried secrets. I've led global change initiatives by day and cried myself to sleep in silence. I've been called powerful and made to feel powerless. However, every version of me contributed to the creation of a seasoned corporate executive and a strategic reinvention coach. I didn't rise by accident. I grew because I had to, and then I chose to rise even higher as a visionary entrepreneur, building businesses that reflect both purpose and power.

I like to say I received an assignment before I was born. My mother, Sally, had fought and won an extraordinary battle with bipolar disorder and schizophrenia. She spent two years in a catatonic state at a psychiatric center.

One day, my mother broke through her catatonia and asked another patient for a puff of their cigarette. Not long after, she was well enough to come home. She surprised my dad when almost her first words to him after coming out of her catatonic state were, "I want to have another baby," despite the fact my two brothers were already teenagers. And she did, at age 36.

My mother's decision created repercussions in my life that I'm sure she never expected. As early as I can remember, I felt it was my responsibility to save her from her mental illness and make her life better. Fortunately, my father's strength anchored my life as well as my mother's health for the first decade of my life. He loved us both unconditionally, and he stood by her through the ups and downs of her mental illness. I learned the value of love and perseverance from both my parents; it was the foundation for much of what I took into my adult life. Their passion for one another and their determination to hold our family together taught me never to give up, no matter what the odds.

Mom never let her mental illness stop her from achieving. She wrote more than 200 songs, with thirteen of those copyrighted and four published. She worked with some of the biggest names in music. Her initiative and resourcefulness were incredible. She chased her purpose with a fire that never quit, and her fire lit something inside of me, too. Mom showed me what it meant to be fearless in the face of adversity and taught me how to dream with a wild, unapologetic heart.

When my dad was diagnosed with amyotrophic lateral sclerosis (ALS), or Lou Gehrig's disease, I was only nine, and it devastated all of us. My mother reversed roles and became his pillar of strength. I watched her nurse him with a level of tenderness and devotion that equaled the years of loving care he'd given her. He was gone just nine months after his diagnosis, and the foundation of my world shifted.

After my dad died, grief and grit filled our home. I watched mom struggle to keep food on the table, saw her bury herself under the blankets for days, and lived through the trauma of her seizures, suicide attempts, and breakdowns.

She never gave up on raising me to the best of her ability, and I knew I was the center of her world, but I often felt that I was raising us both. I became much more than just a daughter. I'd inherited parts of my new role from my dad. I became her confidante, her companion, and far too often her caregiver. I tried to be strong for her every day because I knew she was trying hard to hold it together. It was a tremendous burden for a child, but I wouldn't have had it any other way. I knew we both needed to survive her challenges. I loved her and still do.

Coping with the constant ups and downs and unpredictability of her illness drained and marked me. I wasn't the easiest teenager to be around. I was starting to find my voice and acting out in all the usual ways, such as drinking alcohol and being a little rebellious.

The ongoing financial struggle we had after my dad died was another key stressor in my young life, and it profoundly shaped my values and carved something unshakeable into me. I vowed never to put myself in a position where I had to depend on anyone else for stability or financial survival. That commitment became a defining part of my identity, shaping my ambition and catapulting me forward. It fueled my drive to build an independent and secure life. I didn't just want success; I needed it like oxygen.

Growing up in the Adirondacks, I knew I wanted more than what I saw around me. Of course, the traditional exit strategy was college. I wasn't an exceptional student, and higher education felt financially and academically out of reach. When I was old enough to consider college, I was too rebellious and distracted by my struggles.

Despite my promises to myself, I wasn't on target to reach any of my goals. At age 25, I was broke, divorced, paying a mortgage that cost more than half of my salary, juggling two dead-end jobs, and making barely $13,000 a year. A moment of clarity hit me: *I was going nowhere fast.*

Something inside me shifted. I remembered what I had intuitively realized when I watched my mother struggle on her own: *I am meant for more, but the only person who can change my circumstances is me.* That realization marked a turning point in my life.

I took a leap, landed a temp job at a local phone company, and got my first break. I worked as a customer care consultant in the call center, which I thoroughly enjoyed. My boss, Susan Harrington, saw something in me and gave me a chance to work on an Information Technology (IT) project. This single opportunity lit a spark that would ignite the rest of my life.

Soon, I was sitting down with a 5-by-7-inch yellow-lined pad, scribbling out a plan. My goal was simple yet ambitious: I aimed to earn $100,000 by the time I was 30, less than five years away.

My education became something far more focused than a general college education. I gained knowledge through real-world experiences, earned industry certifications, and built a foundation of self-taught expertise that fueled my success. Though I eventually came within a semester of earning a bachelor's degree from Arizona State University, my most important education was forged in the trenches, leading complex, multimillion-dollar initiatives, cross-functional teams, and navigating high-stakes dynamics of corporate America.

Six months shy of my 30th birthday, I was in California, leading a team of information security professionals at a salary of $105,000 per year for one of the world's most renowned software companies. I met my goal! That moment wasn't just about hitting a number; it was about proving to myself that I could create the life I had dared to dream about. That decision to bet on myself changed everything, and it set me on a successful career trajectory that has taken me around the world, working for Fortune 100 and 500 companies, living in China and Singapore, and building a thriving career I not only enjoyed but took fierce pride in.

While I climbed the corporate ladder, privately, my life painted a different picture and took much longer to make the same switch. I was drowning in toxic, manipulative, abusive love—or what I thought was love.

> "Success is a journey, not a destination."

I got married at 21, in love and full of hope. My first husband didn't start as a monster, but it didn't take long before I was walking on eggshells, bracing for the next rage or the next punishment.

Despite my denial that my marriage was destructive to *me*, I knew I couldn't bring a child into such a dangerous environment. After he threatened me and our unborn child, I had a secret abortion. It was one of the most challenging decisions I've made, but it was the right one for me and the life I was carrying.

One day, in the middle of a fight, he grabbed me by the throat and lifted me off the ground. My legs dangled. His cousin's stepdaughter, just a toddler, stood frozen, watching.

I knew if I didn't leave, I might not make it. I took two weeks to gather my courage and ask my husband for what I euphemistically called "a break." When he agreed, I packed his bags and handed them to him as he walked out the door. The next day, I filed for a restraining order and divorce.

Why didn't I leave sooner? Why did I stay at all? Those are the questions I asked myself for too many years as I continued in a series of toxic relationships, each one as destructive as the last, each one teaching me what love is not. On the surface, everything looked perfect, but behind closed doors, I was navigating the chaos of abusive relationships that few knew existed. Years later, I found myself married again. This time, to a man whose charm was so convincing, I didn't see the trap until I was already inside. He was brilliant, handsome, and a clinically diagnosed narcissist who gaslighted me, twisted my reality, and made me question my strength and sanity. When police arrested him for luring a minor in a sting operation, I stayed. For five more years, I endured constant emotional abuse.

I hid everything—his arrest, his guilty plea, his registered status. I told no one, except my best friend and his family. It felt like an undeniable weight I carried alone.

Why did I stay yet again? Because I thought I could fix him, just like I thought I could fix everyone else. That burning need to heal the broken wasn't new—it was in my DNA. But healing doesn't come from fixing others. It comes from reclaiming yourself. When I realized that, something shifted inside me.

It was like every emotional wound I'd ever carried—the abandonment, the abuse, the bruises you couldn't see—suddenly healed at once. Not perfectly. Not prettily. But powerfully.

In a split second, I didn't just feel my worth—I saw it, standing outside myself, radiant and undeniable. For the first time in my life, I understood:

- I was never meant to fix anyone.
- I wasn't broken; I was becoming.

When I realized all of that and the implications, I threw the television remote control, not in a rage, but in release.

And with a voice that shook with the force of my awakening, I spoke the words that changed everything: GET OUT!

And, just like that, I chose me.

If you've been waiting for a permission slip to choose yourself, THIS IS IT! You don't need anyone else's blessing to rise. You don't need more reasons to leave what's breaking you. YOU are the reason. If you need someone to hand you that permission slip, let me be the one to place it firmly into your hands.

After that epiphany, I focused on myself and became someone with whom a genuinely great person would want to partner. I created space for myself first. I didn't just focus on the relationship I wanted; I focused on the woman I was becoming. I didn't manifest a hero to rescue me. I manifested a partner who could meet me where I stood strong, sovereign, and ready.

And that's when Steve showed up. A professional firefighter, no less. A real-life hero by trade, but by the time he found me, I didn't need saving. I needed someone who could stand in the fire with me.

We've been married for fifteen years, and every day, I'm reminded of what's possible when you heal, choose yourself, and open yourself up to the relationship and joy you deserve. Life constantly challenges us. I don't define my happiness by being with Steve; instead, he enhances the joy and contentment I create within myself.

Before I met him, I had stopped dancing in the living room. As a child, I danced freely, especially when my dad was alive or my mom had a good day. But somewhere along the way, I lost that part of myself. Meeting Steve didn't give it back to me—finding myself did.

Now, I dance in the living room all the time, music blaring, spirit soaring, and celebrating not just the relationship we've built, but the life I've fought for, the woman I've become, and the road I traveled to get here.

Dancing for me is gratitude in motion. Gratitude for my happiness, freedom, and the fierce, unstoppable version of me that rose from the ashes. Happiness and fulfillment are never about titles, paychecks, or even love itself. They're about what those things bring: security, comfort, peace, and joy.

Transformation starts with choices—sometimes small, sometimes seismic. You must choose to believe you deserve more, to bet on yourself, to choose to step toward the life you envision, even when the path ahead terrifies you. It's never one choice; It's choosing yourself repeatedly.

And every brave, messy, heartbroken, hope-fueled choice I made shaped me into the current version of myself: A woman who no longer chases approval and stands firmly in her worth.

One of the most significant changes in my life has been learning to trust my intuition. It had always been there, but for years, I silenced it. The first time I was married, I knew deep down I shouldn't have gone through with it. The signs were there. The voice inside me whispered, "Don't do it." But I told myself it was easier to move forward than to pull the brake. These weren't grand affairs with hundreds of guests or showers of gifts. They were quiet, small weddings. There were no fairy tale moments, just me convincing myself that love, or the idea of it, was enough. Even though I was only ten years old when I lost my father, I believed I knew what he would have wanted for me to hold out for a man who was worthy of his little girl. And before Steve, none of them were.

Learning to trust my intuition didn't happen overnight. I slowly reclaimed the voice I had buried under fear and loneliness. My intuition isn't just a whisper; it's a force. It influences every decision I make, and I trust it without hesitation. It is the compass that keeps me true to myself, no matter how loud the world gets.

Today, I don't live in the past. I don't carry regret like a heavy cloak around my shoulders. I have compassion for the woman I was—a woman who was trying to navigate life, find love, and heal in the only ways she knew how. I've forgiven her because she deserves forgiveness and grace. And I've forgiven those who hurt me, too. Not for them. For me. Forgiveness isn't about excusing what happened; it's about freeing your heart to create a future that isn't chained to an old story. Holding on to pain keeps you tethered to the past. Letting it go sets you free.

Recognizing the most influential people in my life is integral to understanding my journey. And here's the irony: They aren't just the people who loved me; they're also the ones who didn't. Those relationships, as painful as they were, created the unstoppable woman I am today.

My philosophy is simple: Regret, forgiveness, and growth are choices. Every decision, misstep, and moment I wished had gone differently led me to a life that feels aligned, joyful, and mine.

I dislike the word "failure." It feels too final, too narrow, and too small to define the whole arc of a life like mine. Life isn't a pass/fail test; it's a series of lessons. What some people call failures, I see as invitations to grow, pivot, and evolve. That mindset shaped how I approach adversity and setbacks. Success isn't just about winning; it's about how you rise when things fall apart.

> " Legacy isn't what you leave behind. It's what you spark in others while you're still here "

I've started things and not finished them. I didn't complete my bachelor's degree, which many might consider a failure. My decision to focus on non-traditional education set me on a path to prove that a piece of paper doesn't define success. I've built up successful businesses and a thriving career, achieved multi-seven-figure earnings, and worked for some of the world's most respected organizations, all without a college degree. The world's definitions of success and failure don't have to be yours.

Failure isn't about what didn't work; it's about how you faced the wreckage, learned from it, and determined your next move. I've proven to myself that no matter what falls apart, I can and will make the bold move, because even in chaos, I know how to lead the board.

When I was younger, success was simple: the sprawling mansion I sketched in art class and a life that felt grand and far removed from the small-town reality in which I grew up. It wasn't that I didn't love my hometown, but I knew it wasn't where my dreams would thrive. Back then, success meant escaping the familiar, getting a good job, and building a life that looked impressive from the outside. For a while, I chased that version of success relentlessly.

The job I landed at 29½ was working at a Fortune 500 company, earning six figures, managing a team, and occupying a high-rise office with a window. I lived in a cute apartment and felt like I'd made it. That version of success—title, salary, and independence—felt tangible and so validating.

Then, 9/11 hit, and the information technology industry hit a massive downturn. I wasn't just watching the layoffs happen; I was helping to lead them, until one day, I found myself laid off, too. I was devastated. It was a wake-up call I never saw coming. I realized painfully that I had tied my worth to the tangibles—the job, the income, and the title; but they were just achievements. But when it all disappeared, I had to face a truth I'd been running from: the external markers of success might make you feel seen, but they'll never make you feel whole.

At 54, my definition of success has evolved into something more profound and intangible. Today, success is about the life I've built, the peace I feel, the love I share with my husband, and the joy of being surrounded by true friends who treat me with kindness, respect, and genuine care. It's about living in a beautiful home that serves as a sanctuary, filled with love, laughter, and our beloved poodles. Most of all, it's about knowing that I'm at a place in life where I want for nothing. Not because I have everything, but because I finally became everything I once needed.

Success is not a fixed destination. It's a moving force, constantly evolving, continually expanding, just like me. I am and always will be a lifelong learner, reaching for the next thing, driven by the little girl who saw her mother struggle and vowed to create a different life. That motivation still fuels me, but it's no longer about proving myself to the world. It's about fulfilling my purpose and helping others reach their full potential.

If you ask me today if I've succeeded, I'd say yes and no. Yes, I am successful. I've built a life I'm proud of, filled with gratitude, joy, and calm. But success is something you never fully grasp. Striving, learning, and growing make life meaningful. Success is a journey, not a destination.

Success is about balance: striving for greatness while appreciating where I am. It's about joy, resilience, and the ability to create a life that feels whole and complete. It's ever-changing, and it's a privilege to continue defining it as I grow.

The day I fulfilled a promise to my older brother, Bobby, changed me forever. Bobby was the kind of soul who lit up every room he entered—charismatic, funny, handsome, and heartbreakingly human. His struggles with addiction never erased his kindness or his beautiful spirit.

I had promised Bobby he would not die alone. When I arrived at his bedside, Bobby was in a coma, but somehow, he knew I was there. He rallied for a brief, miraculous moment, looked straight at me, and said, "I love you, sis." Those were his last words. When he slipped back into a coma, the doctors turned to me to make the decision I knew was coming.

That night, I held his hand as he took his last breath, overwhelmed by a profound, almost sacred peace. It was one of the most extraordinary experiences of my life. Helping him transition to the other side felt like the mirror image of a mother bringing new life into the world. It was a moment that shifted me, not just emotionally, but spiritually. That experience planted a seed inside me that eventually grew into a deep passion for helping others through profound life transitions. It led me to become an End-of-Life Doula, holding sacred space for those crossing over, and for their loved ones who stay behind. Loss came in waves after that. Two years later, I lost my mother. A decade later, I lost my brother Michael to the same disease that took our father, ALS. Each goodbye left a scar. But each scar also cracked me open in new, beautiful ways. Because with every loss, I found another part of myself.

After Bobby passed, something wild and unexpected stirred in me—an undeniable urge to create. I walked into an art supply store and spent $500 on brushes, paint, and canvas. I didn't know what I was doing—I just knew I had to do it. To my surprise, I discovered a raw, untamed talent for painting. Local galleries and bistros featured my abstract paintings and resin art. People commissioned pieces. They hung my art in their homes. And for the first time in a long time, I realized: Grief didn't just break me. It helped me grow into a fuller, richer version of who I was meant to become. Now, creativity flows through every part of my life—not just in the art I create, but in the lives I help others design as well. Through coaching, healing work, every word I write, and every space I hold. Healing became not just a personal journey, but a sacred calling. As a Reiki Master, ThetaHealer, and Quantum Healing Hypnosis Technique (QHHT) practitioner, I discovered new ways to help others release pain, reconnect with their inner wisdom, and realign with their most authentic selves. I don't just offer traditional coaching. I offer transformational, soul-level healing—helping women rise not just emotionally, but energetically, spiritually, and creatively.

Whether it's helping a woman break free from toxic cycles, guiding her back to her intuition, or holding sacred space as she heals from unseen wounds, I bring every part of myself to the work I do. Because I know firsthand: sometimes the most significant losses crack us open, so the light inside can finally escape.

As I write this chapter, I've considered a few significant moments. One was the launch of my coaching career, when I attended a

Mastermind event featuring Dean Graziosi and Tony Robbins. Without preparation, I was invited to share my story on stage in front of 150 people. For years, I had visualized myself speaking on stage, and suddenly, there I was for the first time. It was humbling and empowering. Soon, I found myself at the Mastermind headquarters, standing in a multi-million-dollar recording studio, filming a welcome video and a sales talk for my business. When I left the studio, I broke into what Oprah would call an ugly cry of overwhelming gratitude and pride. I realized how far I had come and how every decision and challenge had led me to that moment.

> "My decision to focus on non-traditional education set me on a path to prove that a piece of paper doesn't define success."

The legacy I hope to leave isn't a plaque or generational wealth. Legacy is about the ripple effect on how I can continue to inspire and transform lives long after I'm gone. My legacy is the movement I aim to create—a movement that empowers people, especially women, to realize their full potential. Legacy isn't what you leave behind. It's what you spark in others while you're still here.

I want my legacy to be a beacon of hope for those who feel stuck in toxic cycles, whether personal or professional. I remind my clients that healing is possible, and they can rebuild their self-worth and design lives that reflect their purpose, potential, and undeniable power. Everyone deserves to live their life with joy, freedom, and deep fulfillment, and I'm here to help them claim it. Through my coaching, books, speaking engagements, and retreats, I aim to help others recover and thrive far more quickly than it took me. My vision is to help people not only survive their hardships but thrive in their lives, build fulfilling relationships and careers, and realize they are far more capable than they ever believed.

Humor and transparency effectively serve as therapy when life feels heavy. I've learned to laugh and encourage others to do the same, even in the darkest moments. My openness and willingness to discuss my experiences, no matter how personal they may seem, have been my way of connecting with others and finding meaning in adversity. It's a reminder that we're all human and face struggles. I want to inspire others to talk about their struggles by being open about mine.

My legacy is also about creating physical and virtual spaces where transformation happens. I want my retreats to be life-changing, my books to sit on coffee tables as constant reminders of resilience and possibility, and my words to echo in conversations among friends, families, and communities. While many of my events welcome corporate leaders and successful entrepreneurs, they are especially designed for women from all walks of life, those who are rising from setbacks, navigating reinvention, or simply ready to build something meaningful on their own terms.

My legacy is growing and evolving, and I have many years to finish shaping it. What sets it apart from so many others is that it's not just about the result; it's about the lives I can change along the way.

Titles, trophies, or timelines don't measure a legacy. My legacy will be every woman who chooses to prioritize herself.

Legacy is in every heart that beats louder because you refused to stay silent.

It's in every fire sparked by the flames you refused to let die.

You don't leave a legacy by living a perfect life. You leave a legacy by rising bloody, brilliant, and unbreakable and daring others to rise with you.

And that is how you set the whole damn world on fire.

ABOUT BRENDA PETRILLO

Brenda Petrillo is a Strategic Reinvention Coach, women's leadership mentor, and unapologetic force of nature committed to helping executive women reinvent their lives and build powerful new beginnings without sacrificing income, identity, or impact.

With over three decades of experience leading enterprise transformation, people-centered change, and high-impact strategy across Fortune 500 companies, Brenda brings both executive credibility and profound personal wisdom to every client she serves. She knows firsthand what it takes to rise because she's done it, again and again.

After surviving decades of emotionally abusive relationships, including the grip of narcissistic partners, Brenda hit a breaking point that became her breakthrough. She rebuilt her life from the inside out, healing wounds that once held her back, reclaiming her voice, and stepping into her highest calling: to help other women do the same, but in far less time.

Through her signature *Rise and Launch Method*™, she helps women turn adversity into advantage and reinvention into a roadmap for building lives filled with clarity, confidence, and lasting impact.

As the founder of **Anew Phoenix Rising, LLC**, Brenda leads transformational coaching programs, immersive retreats, and ethical AI business accelerators that empower women not to bounce back, but to boldly business what's next, on their terms.

She lives in Arizona with her husband, Steve, the man who honors her fire and dances with her in the living room. Together, they embody what's possible when healing meets wholeness and when a woman finally decides to rise.

 www.anewphoenixrising.com

 brendapetrillo

 BrendaLynnPetrillo

 @anewphoenixrising

 @anewphoenixrising

One Bridge to Healing Your Trauma

CAROL & BRANDON SYLER

*H*ow are you?

This is a deceptively simple question, and most of us answer on autopilot without ever thinking about its real meaning. For most of our lives, the two of us blindly answered as we denied the trauma churning inside us, trauma generated by our fractured childhoods and broken relationships.

So, let's start over. *How are you really? How's your heart?*

This is the basic truth we didn't grasp for far too long: How we're really doing is tied directly to the health of our important, interrelated relationships, and our hearts are the key. A healthy, loving relationship with God leads to a healthy relationship with ourselves, which is a prerequisite for a healthy, loving relationship with others. We learned this the hard way, unfortunately.

Having learned many lessons the hard way, we are now in a position to help you with a better way to heal both your hearts and your most-important relationships.

From the beginning of our marriage, our hearts were damaged and fragmented. When we finally found each other, we married just three months after we met, without taking time to establish a strong foundation. We leaped into a tumultuous, if loving, relationship with much more intensity than intimacy, and without a clue about the damaging baggage we brought along.

When Brandon realized he needed help to overcome chaos at work, he contacted a business coach who asked, "If you want your business to change, what has to change first?" We learned change starts from the inside and spent the next few years rebuilding and healing our hearts, our marriage, and our family as well as the business. Importantly, we also learned God needed to be an integral part of all aspects of our lives.

Rebuilding whole, healthy relationships wasn't a short or easy journey. During the process, we found the tools we needed, and they worked incredibly well to expedite and improve our spiritual and emotional growth. After much thought and prayer, we've decided our mission is to help others discover areas of disconnection that interface with their most important relationships. These areas often point to wounds or false beliefs about God, themselves, others, or the future. We're convinced the best way to do this is to make these tools available through our Sacred Impact program, our faith-based experiential therapy workshop.

Recently we endowed a 501(c)(3) nonprofit, One Bridge, to run the workshops using the best Christian therapists on the planet. Our customized multi-day workshops help anyone unearth the areas of disconnection and pain they've been experiencing for years, and their healing and rebuilding is within a framework of God's grace and love. If they're open and willing, they will unlock new levels of awareness, understanding, compassion, and resilience.

The name *One Bridge* was inspired by a scriptural reference, John 17, in which Jesus prayed for Oneness, for us to be one heart and mind, in connection with each other and Him. This is especially appropriate because Jesus taught through experiential encounters, not lectures.

We use His example to help our workshop participants identify what blocks them from connection, setting the stage to make amends and move toward reconciliation and healing.

We're sharing our stories because there's beauty in the imperfections we recognize and redemption in the pain we've experienced. Although our childhood homes were far from perfect, we love our parents and have compassion for the lives they've lived and the struggles they carried before we came along.

Carol wasn't brought up in a Christian home, but she always had an unspoken belief in God that gave her some internal strength; her mother remembers Carol attended Christian daycare as a young child. Her earliest memories have a faint background of Bible songs and stories, and they comforted her in dark times when she was in pain or alone.

Growing up in a dysfunctional and chaotic home in Colorado, she had many of those dark moments, and she carried her damaged feelings and reactions with her well into her adult years. Her father was a Vietnam veteran with trauma of his own and struggled with alcoholism. He was abusive to her mother, her brother, and her, and his infidelities and addiction to pornography were disruptive forces in their lives.

Carol never felt secure and safe within her family. Her happiest and safest moments were with her horse, Cimmeron, which she was given when she was ten and trained herself. The horse gave Carol the love and safety she'd been missing. Every afternoon she'd take long, solitary rides far from the anger and abuse at home. She trained Cimmeron well enough to ride in competitive gymkhanas, and one year they won the trophy for high point rider and horse of the year.

When she was 15, Carol suffered a tremendous blow when her mother lost her job and they had to sell Cimmeron—she felt as though she'd lost her world. Over the next couple of years, she dropped out of high school and married, and she managed to earn her GED, work her way through school without financial assistance, and graduate from college at the top of her class with honors. Now Carol is semi-retired from a real estate career and directs most of her energy to One Bridge.

As young adults, both of us carried our families' dysfunctions into our marriages. Her trauma and pain had not ended with her childhood. In addition to the sexual abuse she survived as a teen, as an adult she survived physical and sexual assaults, as well as emotional abuse.

Carol divorced her first husband when she was 21 and remarried at 32, this time to an abusive alcoholic like her father. She recycled her childhood traumas as she watched the abuse level escalate and her husband sink into alcoholism. His violence reached a peak when he held her by her neck against the refrigerator. He ripped the phone out of her hands when she escaped and tried to dial 9-1-1, and he knocked their four-year-old off the couch in a rage. Carol grabbed her and ran, barefoot and in her pajamas to her neighbors, Tom and Amanda, whom she barely knew. They didn't hesitate—they rescued her.

Tom and Amanda called the police, comforted Carol and her daughter, and gave them a safe place to sleep. She still gets emotional every time she thinks about what they did for her. They didn't just help in a moment of crisis—they led her on a new path.

They also became the close family she'd always wished for. When Carol joined them at their church, she wept through every service, realizing that healing was possible through Christ. Every word, every song spoke directly to her, and she was soon baptized.

Carol knows dedicating her life to Christ was the most pivotal moment in her life. She'd been searching, full of pain, trying to find meaning, identity, and love, but nothing else had filled the void in her life. Her new friends at church became her extended family, and the love and support she received from them, as well as Tom and Amanda, helped Carol rebuild her life from the ground up.

Brandon's childhood experiences were as painful as well, leading him to become bitter, resentful, angry, and lonely. His family lived in Houston when he was young. Both parents worked long hours, and he was a latchkey kid, spending much time alone, feeling unseen and sometimes unappreciated. His parents had occasional loud, dramatic fights, and he knew far too much about their marital problems and codependency. Brandon realizes they did the best they could.

Fortunately, he also had the benefit of a loving relationship with his grandfather, who became a missionary to the Philippines. Some of his happiest childhood memories are of spending time at the lakeside cottage his grandfather built, in the shade of the East Texas pine trees, down by the water. His parents taught him to love reading, and his hunger to learn through reading has been a lifelong strength and source of wisdom and knowledge. They also taught him the value of hard work and being part of a team. He played baseball and football for most of his school years. When he reached college, not being part of a team sport created a void he filled with alcohol, marijuana, and unhealthy relationships.

In 2008, Brandon was in Wisconsin with a good job as regional manager for a parts company, still married to his first wife and living with their young son and daughter. When the recession ended his job, he thought being laid off was a positive sign because he always had a dream of having a business of his own, and he launched his own distribution business from his garage.

Later that year, his father lost *his* job as well, and he joined Brandon as a partner in his new business. When both parents moved in with Brandon's family, his already rocky marriage was strained even further.

Brandon was able to escape the escalating stress with his marriage and parents by adding an export division to the business and traveling for months at a time in Central and South America. Despite this, his relationship with his wife continued to deteriorate almost as fast as his business grew. His parents moved to the Carolinas to establish new headquarters for the company, and he and his wife moved to Georgia to set up another business location in Atlanta.

Despite the moves, the marriage didn't survive. After his divorce, Brandon moved to the Carolinas to be near family. He wasn't doing well mentally, emotionally, or spiritually, and he numbed his pain with overwork, alcohol, and unhealthy relationships with women.

We met in 2012 while we were still recovering from our all-too-recent divorces—Brandon's first and Carol's second. We fell hard for each other, and without thinking about the consequences, we were married within three months. We did our best to blend our two girls and a boy into one happy family, but our kids had been hurt by years of turmoil and tension as our former marriages fell apart. They had no chance to recover before we created a new family shaped by our unreasonable expectations.

Brandon also had made the mistake of sharing information about his marriage difficulties with his children, personal things he should never have told them, exactly as his mother had done with him when he was very young. His indiscretion caused an additional rift with his children, putting them in the middle between his ex-wife and himself.

Our lives didn't magically improve with a new marriage, no matter how much we loved each other. All the problems and chaos that had plagued us for the last few years were still in play, disrupting the business and damaging our new family dynamics. Brandon was fixated on blame and external problems at home and at work, blind to their connection to his internal turmoil. Finally, he realized his business needed help from a professional coach, devouring books on business management as he looked for guidance.

When *E-Myth Revisited* particularly impressed him, he hired

Steve, an E-Myth-certified business coach, to help him put the business aspect of his life in order. Then Steve upended this plan when he asked Brandon a bombshell question: "If your business is going to change, what has to change first?"

Steve's question rocked Brandon, but after pondering it for days, he began to wonder about the impact his own inner turmoil made on his life and business. He signed up for a week-long therapeutic workshop, where he had a series of monumental breakthroughs, and realized the answer to Steve's question was, *If I want my most important relationships to change, **I** must change first.* He continued therapy back home, and the insights he gained began to improve both our marriage and business. Brandon also found a mentor who's still with him, helping him through the many changes he's experienced during 10 years of one-to-one therapy.

Brandon eventually discovered that experiential therapy was particularly effective for overcoming his woundedness; it heals through actions, such as working through hurtful memories. The simplest definition of experiential therapy is, "Anything I can tell, I can show." *Storywork* is the reconciliation of our stories. *Experiential storywork* is working through our pain in a group setting or in a one-on-one setting with a counselor, mentor, sponsor, coach, or friend.

One of Brandon's first storywork experiences relived a Saturday when he was five years old. He remembered feeling *worth less than* and *alone* for the first time, emotions that continued to affect him as a middle-aged adult. In his memory, his mother and father had been at work all week, and when the weekend finally arrived, they didn't get together as a family. Instead, he was alone in his room. His dad was away for the weekend with his fishing buddies, and his mom was busy taking care of his newborn sister.

In an experiential group setting with the guidance of an incredible clinician, others played the roles of his parents. Brandon was able to talk to his "parents" using the voice and words he didn't have when he was five. He finally realized that he *hadn't* been alone; God had been with him then and had never left him.

Like many of us, Brandon was convinced everyone else must have had a harder life than his own. Though he was convinced the trauma he'd gone through was uniquely his, he'd denied the extent of his pain for his entire life. Over the next few days in the workshops, he sat in the groups, hearing other people's stories, and finally mustered up the courage to share his.

Learning *"I'm not alone"* and *"I'm enough!"* made a big impact on Brandon. As he opened up, he was surprised to realize just how disconnected, depressed, and anxious he really was. He began to understand how the wounds from his past negatively impacted his relationship with God, others, and himself. He recognized why he was using contempt, criticism, defensiveness, blame, and unfair comparisons in his daily dealings with people. Of course, this workshop was just the beginning of the work he needed to do.

Brandon learned that his experiences were not unique, and he and the others in the group worked through their pain experientially and together. He also learned that connecting with the stories of others and walking with them through their pain helps us heal, and he's pouring into others, finding it integral in his own healing journey.

In Carol's case, she'd survived by blocking and refusing to recognize her pain; she'd never discuss what happened or how she'd been damaged. She cut off any probes with a dismissive, "Oh, why do people live in their past? Just move on with your life." Within the safety of guided experiential therapy sessions, Carol finally knew she could trust others. When she opened up and acknowledged what had happened to her and how it had affected her, she finally began to heal.

Over the last 10 years, we've both attended experiential workshops with world-renowned clinicians. While in a safe environment, we work through difficult times in our lives. Healing begins as the impact of each wound is named, relationships begin to be reconciled, and false beliefs are replaced with truth.

Much of our therapy over the last 10 years has been working with some of the best Christian clinicians in the world such as Jim Cress and Laurie Lokey. While there are many types of modalities and workshops available, few are experiential, intensive, Christ-centered, and done in a group.

Because we've experienced its immense value, we decided to make it available to the world. Creating awareness of experiential therapy and inspiring others to start or continue their own storywork became our focus. Thanks to the success of the business Brandon founded, we had the resources to set up a nonprofit just over a year ago.

> "There's a hole in our soul that only God can fill."

One Bridge offers an immersive, Christ-centered retreat to help people identify areas of disconnection interfering with their most important relationships. Our workshops can be customized for groups as small as 4 and as large as 40. Most of the work for the week is done in smaller groups of 4 to 8 people led by a world-renowned clinician experienced in facilitating experiential group exercises.

Workshops can be customized for business teams, first responders, veterans, or specific groups or be a combination of people from different walks of life. Our workshops can also be customized for couples who aim to learn each other's stories and deepen their compassion and understanding for their spouse. However, we urge couples to do their own individual work first because there must be a "me" before there can be a "we."

In our workshops, our clients identify and explore patterns of self-sabotage and areas of disconnection within themselves. They'll explore some of the strategies that have developed throughout their life experiences that are impacting their most important relationships.

There's an old saying in Christian recovery groups: "There's a hole in our soul that only God can fill." We believe many relationships carry holes or tears that also need repair. Sometimes the rip comes from words spoken by someone we love—messages such as *You're not enough, What's wrong with you,* or *You'll never amount to anything.* Other times the message is never spoken out loud, but it's sent by criticism, comparison, or neglect.

In response, we develop coping strategies. One person may chase achievement—climbing in education or hustling up the corporate ladder in search of worth. Another may try to fill the emptiness with food, alcohol, or other distractions. Yet these coping strategies often deepen the separation in our relationships, leaving wounds that still need to be reconciled and repaired.

Our Sacred Impact Program at One Bridge delivers months of traditional weekly therapy in 3-5 days. Investing 7-10 hours a day for a week is like spending several months in therapy using the traditional one-on-one, 1 hour per week model.

Purely by time invested, 7-10 hours per day equals several months spent with a counselor in the traditional 1 hour per week model. Now take the wisdom of our world class counselors, working through your own work with others, helping others work through their stories and at times, observing, and you have an immersive experience designed to accelerate breakthrough in a safe environment removed from distraction.

It's human to have fears and reservations about attending any type of workshop where a group of people will be discussing their lives and emotions. The results depend on the attendees' willingness to engage in an open, honest, and vulnerable way.

We're only as sick as our secrets and keeping secrets, downplaying our stories, and even blocking out parts of them, have been part of our journey. Today, as we continue our storywork, we're very open to sharing our stories and coping strategies that have worked against us hurting our relationships and our new & improved strategies for healing them. The old saying really is true...Hurt people hurt people and healing people heal people.

The health of our families, workplaces, and communities depend on a commitment to reality at all costs. As we work through the weight of our pain dragging us down and holding us back, our load lightens up and our capacity increases for others. We're more present with our families, our workplaces, our communities, and beyond. People are attracted to us and drawn in. Our influence ripples through the world as we walk with others through their pain. This is why we call our program Sacred Impact.

When we keep our stories hidden inside, they can't do anybody any good. Since she's become aware of the value of her stories, Carol has become very open to others hearing them, including our children. As a teen, our daughter said, "Mom, how could you understand? You've never done anything bad in your life."

Carol looked at her and said, "Oh, honey, let me tell you about my past. I don't want you to make the same mistakes I made." Since then, they've talked about sex, abortions, marriage, self-esteem, and relationship violence, and no subjects are off limits.

We began holding our retreats in Dobson, North Carolina, overlooking the Blue Ridge Mountains, and had commissioned plans to build our own facility. One of our retreat attendees connected us with the WinShape Foundation, a Christian charitable organization founded by Truett and Jeanette Cathy, the couple who founded Chick-fil-A. That connection opened the door for us to be able to run our Sacred Impact Program at WinShape's retreat in Rome, Georgia. As we changed our focus from building our own site to our programming and transforming hearts and lives, opportunities at several other places began to emerge.

Another couple have gifted the use of their beautiful homes on an Oklahoma lake to One Bridge. With access to these spectacular locations, we're beginning to build customized intensive workshops for various groups, increasing access to a wider variety of retreats.

One Bridge retreats begin on Monday evenings with a warm welcome for up to 40 participants. While some people are nervous, most are excited to get away for the week to a resort-like setting and they have high expectations. We're there, too, mostly behind the scenes, but also serving as hosts and facilitators, doing our best to put everyone at ease.

Our first goal is to help them understand they're in a *safe* zone. We have dinner and then set the tone for the week. Brandon shares his story of the chaos he experienced at work and at home, and how experiential group exercises helped him create more capacity for the people in his life and inspired him to continue working through the trauma and false beliefs from his past. From here, we run through some fun connection exercises as a large group and set the tone for the week.

In the morning after breakfast, there's often a special surprise presentation at the horse arena. After the morning kickoff, the participants separate into small groups of six to eight, each group with their own therapist, and move into cozy living room environments on campus.

Each clinician has their own version of a check-in exercise. One example is where the participants choose to stand close to a sign that says most closely how they're feeling at that moment (mad, glad, sad, bad, or afraid) and share why they've chosen to stand near that sign. It creates connection and safety because people empathize with each other and have a gauge for where they are and where others are in the room.

Each group of eight has a flip chart, and they use it to write down their own group rules. The clinicians have a few nonnegotiable stipulations to head up the list: *Everything said in this room will be held in strictest confidence; we use only first names; we don't share what we do for a living.* At that point, the group members hash out the rest of their own rules.

The purpose is to build a safe environment where people can allow themselves to become vulnerable. Mutual trust is the indispensable "secret sauce" for success. Openness, honesty, and vulnerability are important in all of the workshops. In our customized couples' intensives, it is of great value to the relationship to learn each other's stories and connect the dots to current circumstances and future hopes and dreams. When open and committed to reality, couples leave our customized intensives with more compassion and empathy for one another.

> "The world is in the middle of a global mental health pandemic."

We include *bibliodrama*, an experiential way of entering a biblical narrative inviting participants to step into the story, explore emotions, and encounter Christ in a transformational way.

With experiential therapy, people play roles in others' lives or just observe. For instance, in Brandon's scenario with his mother and father, two others took the roles of his parents, and he was finally able to say the words he wasn't able to say 45 years before. As an older and wiser version of himself (and guided and facilitated by the clinician), he spoke truths that he'd held back for those decades. He didn't realize the depth of his pain until he began to speak to his parents. Everyone else shared that moment with him, silently but with empathy and support, some even gaining additional insight into their own parental stories.

Whether they hope to be better spouses, parents, ministers, leaders, or coaches, every person attending a retreat is almost certain to leave with additional tools for growth. Group members spend this time learning about each other, building trust and a sense of community, and forging lifelong bonds. The workshops are places for healing and renewal. Retreats end on Friday morning with prayers, discussion, breakfast, and farewells.

Most of us don't acknowledge or deal with our own damaged hearts, much less work at healing them. Instead, we haul them along as baggage into our most intimate and important relationships. We've learned when we don't work through our pain, trauma, and false beliefs, we'll carry the weight and negatively impact the people around us with contempt, blame, comparison, defensiveness and more. The damage continues from marriage to marriage and from generation to generation. We can personally vouch for that!

As part of our journey to better mental, emotional, and spiritual health, the two of us make conscious efforts to forgive both others and ourselves. We've learned not to sweep mistakes under the rug, whether they're ours or someone else's. We choose love, forgiveness, and conciliation. There's not enough of those in the world, and all are needed now, more than ever.

We've learned the vital importance of forgiveness and making amends with our loved ones. We realize that keeping family bonds strong by healing the rips and tears in our relationships is essential, reaching beyond just our own homes. Strong family bonds impact our workplaces, our communities, and even the legacy we leave behind. They strengthen our hearts and build resilience.

Forgiveness may be the most important step many of us take. Learning to forgive deeply was a long journey for us. Now forgiveness is like oxygen—unseen yet essential—something we breathe in and breathe out as we extend it to others.

The world is in the middle of a global mental health pandemic. The two of us want to raise awareness and set the table for God to heal through our intensives including our Sacred Impact Program.

We want our legacy to be one of positive impact on the lives of others, sharing our mission and vision, and making a positive change impacting generations.

The good news is that there's a healthy way for our hearts to be healed. It takes courage, safety, trust, determination, and yes, an act of God.

ABOUT CAROL & BRANDON SYLER

Carol and Brandon Syler dedicate their time and substantial assets to their faith-based 501(c)(3) nonprofit, One Bridge. Their mission is to help others discover areas of disconnection that are interfering with their most important relationships, including their connection to God.

Through experiential therapy, *Storywork*, and the care of outstanding Christian clinicians, the Sylers and One Bridge host customized multi-day for individuals and couples seeking deeper healing. Their Sacred Impact retreats create a safe place to explore personal stories, address barriers that interfere with healthy communication and connection, and begin the work of restoration. Attendees gain greater understanding of the impact of their stories and identify areas blocking them from healthy communication and connection. Each retreat is supported with practical resources and thoughtful follow-up care plans to help participants continue their journey toward lasting healing.

Carol Syler was raised in Colorado, where she trained her horse, Cimmeron, competed in gymkhanas, and went on long horseback rides to escape a dysfunctional home. She survived sexual abuse, rapes, and physical violence in her youth and early adulthood, coping with her pain by denying or ignoring it. Despite not finishing high school, Carol worked her way through college and graduated with honors. She worked as a dental hygienist and then as a real estate agent before committing her time to One Bridge.

Brandon was raised and attended college in Texas. During the 2008 Great Recession, he launched a parts distribution business in Wisconsin before relocating its headquarters to South Carolina. His personal journey toward healing led him through years of therapy as he sought to understand the roots of his anger, bitterness, and criticism, eventually discovering the transformative impact of experiential therapy and *Storywork*. Today, Brandon is committed to raising awareness of storywork and helping people deepen their closest relationships so they can have an exponential impact in their families, workplaces, and communities.

Brandon and Carol have three adult children, Landry, Parker, and Lindsay. They reside in Tega Cay, South Carolina, and enjoy exploring nature and playing golf and pickleball in their spare time.

 Onebridgeexperience.com

 Mpparts.com

 One Bridge

 @OneBridgeExperience

Attitude is Everything

CURT HAVENS

My life has been wonderful, wildly successful, and much better than I could have dreamed when I was a middle-class kid growing up in New England. Unfortunately, my happiness and success didn't zoom straight upward by any stretch of the imagination. I crashed and burned in my mid-thirties, and it took me six years to find my way back, rebuild my family, and start a new business.

What I learned on both my way up and my way down may be helpful to you, and I'm grateful to share my hard-earned knowledge. I hope you can learn a few lessons from a self-made man, someone who has spent a significant portion of his life trying to accomplish what everyone said was impossible.

I'm the oldest child in a large, tightly knit, hardworking family living about 17 miles north of Boston, Massachusetts. My grandfather was Rensselaer Curtiss Havens Sr., my father was Jr., and I am III, although I've always been known by the name Curt. We moved from New York State to settle permanently in the idyllic harbor town of Marblehead soon after I was born. My mother was a waitress before becoming a real estate agent, and my dad owned a small construction company.

Dad worked hard and was an incredible contractor, but we never became well-off, mainly because he was such a kind and generous person. He always went above and beyond, seldom charged what he should have for the changes people requested.

Marblehead was a great place to grow up in the '60s and '70s, a wholesome small town that was just off the beaten path enough to keep us out of too much trouble. Life wasn't always easy for me. I stuttered when I was young and was bullied. I was a mediocre student, five feet, four inches tall and 100 pounds at age 16, far too small for football or any of the other high school sports that offered recognition and glory. I finally found my niche in gymnastics, where I excelled. In high school, I didn't make a powerful impression on my classmates. I had friends, but I wasn't particularly popular or outgoing.

We never had money for any extras, so all five of us kids worked to fund our hobbies and luxuries. I was a strong and hardworking little kid from the time I started my newspaper route at the age of 10. When I was big enough, I worked for my dad in construction. I laugh that I grew up swinging a hammer, but it's true; I learned how to build things at a very young age. The skills my dad taught me have helped me all my life, and they were the first building block to my success as an adult.

It took a lot of work to fund my champagne tastes, because from the time I was a toddler, I loved airplanes and wanted to fly. My grandfather inspired me. The first Rensselaer Curtiss Havens was a superb pilot and an aviation pioneer, not just another weekend warrior. When he was young, Grandfather was a barnstormer, one of those death-defying aerobatic daredevils. When he gave up aerobatics, he became one of the first pilots to fly DC-3s for American Airlines.

As a future aviator, I was determined to earn my private pilot's license immediately after obtaining my driver's license. Flying came naturally to me, and I soloed after just eight hours. For luck, I had taken Grandfather's wings off their decorative plaque and pinned them under my lapel. I still remember yelling *"Yahoo!"* as I took off on my first solo flight. It was a wicked good feeling made even sweeter because I had paid for every moment of it myself.

My goal was to be appointed to the Air Force Academy, but I had yet-undiagnosed Attention Deficit/Hyperactivity Disorder (ADHD) and had trouble concentrating on my studies. With my mediocre grades, I needed to earn stellar Scholastic Aptitude Test (SAT) scores, but taking tests wasn't my strength. After graduating from high school in 1978, I attended a military-style prep academy in Oregon from September to March. The focus was on elevating our SAT scores, and I took the math and English tests every month for six months. Though my SAT scores were now in the 90th percentile, they weren't enough to offset the rest of my high school career. I finally accepted that the Air Force Academy wasn't in my future. I didn't have a backup plan, but when my girlfriend headed to Arizona State University (ASU), I followed her.

I knew I had to pay for college myself, and the out-of-state tuition was steep. When my parents questioned why I made that choice, I reassured them I could handle the expenses, and of course, being at the same school as my girlfriend was pure coincidence, but they weren't buying it.

My first semester at ASU was beyond miserable:

- My girlfriend dumped me just three weeks into the semester.
- I didn't know anybody.
- I was living off-campus in a deplorable rented room.
- I worked many hours each week, bagging groceries to pay rent and tuition.
- I was as poor as a church mouse.
- I was horrifically homesick for my siblings and parents.
- I was enrolled as an engineering major, which I discovered I hated.
- I was too stubborn to admit my move to Arizona was a bad idea.

I was happy to be going home for Christmas. I didn't want to go back to Arizona, but I also had no desire to prove my parents right. I am a fairly religious person, and it was natural for me to close my eyes, lean my head against the airplane window, and pray, *"God, please put something in my path that will change the semester and make it a good one."* I cried and prayed that thought the entire flight.

The only true joy was my beloved motorcycle. My grandmother, Mimi, helped me buy it and told me, "It is our secret." My parents would have had a fit.

I'd made one friend in my engineering classes, and when I called to announce I was back in town, he said, "Well, the fraternities are having parties, so let's meet."

It sounded like a good idea, so I hopped onto my motorcycle and somehow drove to the wrong frat house. I was sure I was at the right one because I was greeted at the door and welcomed into a party, and felt so much at home, I never tried to find my friend. I stayed all evening and went back to the house the next day for a barbecue, and I was invited to rush the fraternity. As soon as I pledged, I moved into the frat house to live for the rest of my college career. I'd found my brothers and my Arizona family. It was an immediate answer to my prayer.

Joining the fraternity was a life-defining moment. I gained confidence, leadership skills, and improved communication, transitioning from a relatively shy boy to an outgoing young man— essential attributes for future success. I became the social chairman, ran fundraisers for several nonprofits, and broadened my perspective on life. My brothers in Phi Kappa Psi remain an essential and positive part of my life, forty-five years later.

An oversized pivot and another defining moment was changing my major from engineering to marketing, which I loved. It became another key to my success as an entrepreneur and helped in every aspect of each business I started. Marketing has served me well for my entire life. My happiness quotient increased even further when I found a better full-time job in telemarketing. I was good at sales.

With my career and social life settled, I dug in and made the most of my years at ASU. Because I was paying my way through school and my living expenses, I was only able to take 3-4 classes per semester.

That put me on a five-year schedule, but the time I invested laid an excellent foundation for the rest of my life. It took me years to pay off my student loans in full, but I did it.

My first wife, Aline, and I married right out of college. When I graduated, my employer offered me a permanent job in telemarketing, but I believed I could do more with my life. We moved back east to Marblehead to join my family's construction business.

It felt good to work with my dad and brothers again. Everything about houses had always appealed to me. I didn't have much money for a down payment, but I read a book on how to buy real estate for no money down and soon began flipping houses on the side. At only 25, my first flip was perfect. The condo market was booming, and I came across a four-family building that I purchased for $185,000 with no money down, intending to renovate it using my construction skills. Another developer approached me, offered me $245,000 just weeks later, and made a cool $60,000 by just flipping paper. I never actually bought it; they just assumed my position. It was so sweet!

> **"** I was terrified, as you can imagine. Filming in real time is a nerve-wracking experience, especially when you know millions of eyes are on you. **"**

After a few years, we moved 30 miles up the coast to Newburyport, and I continued flipping houses. While working there, I met two men who ran a television program out of the local cable facility. I began to help them out here and there and quickly became fascinated by the video/television (TV) business. When they decided their lives were too full to continue the show, I took it over with their permission and expanded the video production to include weddings and small commercials. Because I volunteered at the cable facility, they allowed me to use the equipment for personal use, and the studio facility became my editing bay.

As I delved deeper into the TV experience, I purchased my own equipment and relocated back to Marblehead. My dad and brothers were building decks, replacing windows, and upgrading houses; I instantly put my construction talents to use and decided to film a small home improvement show.

The demand for this type of show wasn't even on the radar yet. Adding a wood deck onto the back of your house was a relatively inexpensive and very popular improvement, so *How to Build a Deck* was the first episode of my TV series, *Home Improvement Magazine.*

We taped 75 episodes and developed a successful formula, utilizing homes under renovation. I was host and producer, and Russ Barry and Michael Dynice joined me as cameraman and editor. Later, Richard Pinkham became a co-host. A regional chain of home improvement stores sponsored the show and paid the bills.

Television was a fascinating business, and I learned everything I could about what was on the air and how it got there. My show aired on the local cable station, but I yearned for the Boston market, although I knew it would be hard to break into. The only other home improvement program on the air at that time was *This Old House,* hosted by Bob Vila, a PBS show. Though it had higher production values than mine, I did the best I could with the equipment I could afford, and my final product was impressive.

In the process of distributing my show, I found my first mentor, one of the most influential people in my life. Bill Spitzer was the general manager of WQTV, Channel 68, an independent Boston station. He took my show and broadcast it on Sunday mornings, the perfect time to watch a home improvement show back then.

Jeopardy!, The Wheel of Fortune, all the daytime talk shows, and other independent productions are marketed to individual stations by middlemen —companies that do nothing else. The convention of the

National Association of Television Production Executives (NATPE) was held that year in New Orleans. I used my frequent flyer miles and flew there for the event. It was incredible to mingle with the independent producers, who brought the stars of their shows to the convention to dazzle. That's when I learned how TV show syndication worked and used it as a springboard for future endeavors.

When I got home, I told Bill Spitzer I intended to syndicate my show nationally. He said, "Curt, you need to hire a company to do it. I've never seen an unknown producer market a TV show on their own."

"Bill, I *know* I can do it! I have this vision, and I want to try," I said with complete confidence. His voice telling me *this wasn't going to work this way* was loud and clear, I ignored his advice. I'm stubborn; when someone say I can't do something, it lights a fire under me.

At that point, my mind was convinced I was going to get it done and prove him wrong. It wasn't an ego thing, for I had a vision. I knew that if I followed the vision I had created, one step at a time, I would be successful, utilizing a combination of passion and perseverance. This was the foundation of my master plan, serving as my guidebook for success. I'll give you the steps for this plan later in this chapter.

As it turned out, I was right. I syndicated my show out of my basement in Marblehead, just a 31-year-old stubborn guy with limited experience, figuring it out as he went along, determined to succeed, with a show nobody else had. It didn't take long before my show started to be seen on other independent stations, as well as major network stations. Then, things picked up, and stations began calling me directly to license my show. That wasn't the usual way of doing business.

I now had the first nationally syndicated and independently produced home improvement show in the country. HGTV was not even a thought in someone's mind at that point. I was a Pioneer! Soon, it was airing in Chicago, one of the biggest television markets, a real coup. I was in my condo's basement office in February 1992, and I got a call: "This is David Boal from the Oprah Winfrey show."

I hesitated for a split second and said, "Get the f*** out of here," dropping a rare F-bomb. I thought somebody was playing a prank on me. He said, "No, seriously. I'm looking for Curt. One of our producers saw your show, and it's being aired here in Chicago. Oprah is hosting a show on home improvement, and we'd like to know if you'd be interested in flying out to be a guest expert on her show. I haven't seen your show yet, and I'd like to see a segment before we commit."

I couriered him a tape, and the next day, a Thursday, he called me back. "Curt, you're perfect. Are you available to fly out here Sunday with only three days' notice?"

"Yes, I can do that!"

"Here's the itinerary. We're going to fly you out on Sunday, and on Monday, we'll take you to one of the local home improvement centers here in Chicago to get what supplies you need. Meanwhile, I want you to think of a couple of things that you can stage quickly and show an audience within Oprah's format."

Since I was hosting and producing my show, I had some idea of what he was asking me to do, given the time constraints. We had 45 minutes to do a few quick DIY jobs, such as replacing a screen or fixing a broken floor tile. I flew out to Chicago, and on Monday, an associate producer took me shopping for what I needed for the next day's taping.

On the days Oprah filmed, she taped two shows a day, one at 11 a.m. and one at 1 p.m. She only broadcasts five shows a week, but they needed extras *"in the can"* for future shows, so she and the staff stay ahead of the curve. I went to Harpo Studios, taped the show at 11 a.m. that Tuesday, and was out by noon.

In 1992, Oprah had a daily audience of 20 million people. Before I went on, I stood behind the scenes, watching from a distance as the studio audience entered and was seated, then watching Oprah from a distance backstage, talking with another producer. David Boal was rubbing my shoulders and telling me, "Relax, you're gonna be great." I remember Oprah waving at me just before taping as she quickly ran down the hall to the ladies' room. I don't remember much about the taping after that—it was a blur. I was terrified. Filming in real time is a nerve-wracking experience, especially when you know millions of eyes are on you.

I'm very critical of how I do things, and when I watched the show, I thought I'd done well but could have done better. I didn't make any horrible mistakes, and I doubt people could see how nervous I was, but I was embarrassed to watch it again when it finally aired. Twenty million people watched, and my phone rang off the hook.

> "Don't be overwhelmed by the big picture; keep your focus by taking the task incrementally."

My 15th high school class reunion was the following year, and many of my classmates had seen the show. For a kid who was a nonentity during my four years of school, I finally had my 15 minutes of fame.

After my appearance on Oprah, Bill called and gave me the biggest compliment of all, a life-defining moment.

"I'm calling to apologize, Curt. I doubted you, and I said you couldn't do it that way. You proved me wrong. You're one in a million, and very few people could do what you did. I'm glad I took a chance on you, and I'm proud of you," he said.

For someone whom I admire to give me such a glowing compliment gave me incredible confidence, and it stayed with me. It changed my life forever and for the better. I knew I could do anything.

Things were going great right up to the moment when it all crashed around me. Within a year, my life began to fall apart. My marriage ended in 1993, and the divorce was finalized in November 1994. Aline opted to return to Arizona to be back with her family. When I realized my kids would be across the country, I knew I had to go West as well.

My life quickly imploded, and for several years, I struggled. Family is vital to my well-being. The divorce hurt my daughter and two sons. My bond with them was strained at first, but I worked hard rebuilding my relationship with them and my ex-wife. I was barely able to pay the bills. My credit rating was in the toilet. For several years, I was in a really dark place. It was the most challenging time of my life.

Though I was never diagnosed with clinical depression, I knew I had all of the symptoms, and in retrospect, I'm sure that was my problem. After a long time of not feeling like myself, I walked into a business and saw a giant poster shouting, "*Attitude is Everything!*" It spoke directly to me. I was given a few bumper stickers with the same saying and placed them all over my lonely apartment to remind me what I had to do to get out of this funk. From that moment, I made a conscious effort to maintain a positive attitude towards everything I did. After several years, I was able to pull myself out of the murky waters.

That time in my life is nothing I'd wish on my worst enemy, but everything happens for a reason. Though the dark times almost sank me, you must hit bottom before you can reach the top. You must hit those lows to fully enjoy the highs.

I still owned my video equipment and was producing a kids' show in which I had a part interest. Eventually, I sold my interest in the show for $125,000 and paid off all of my debt, which was a massive burden off my shoulders. After that, I sold insurance for a couple of years.

In 2000, I met Natalie and had my third life-defining moment. I realized I had to get my act together if I was going to have a chance with her. I knew this bright, beautiful teacher deserved a lot more than I had to give at that time. She was a divorced single mother of one son, and as a teacher, she'd seen some challenging blended-family scenarios. She knew what I'd been going through and had doubts about me and my ability to create a good, stable life for us and all four of our kids. She was the type of person who despised debt; her house was even paid for. I sure wasn't in that position, yet.

I kept trying to convince her that I was climbing an anthill, not a mountain, and she could trust me. I knew she was the person I wanted to spend the rest of my life with.

A close friend who worked for a large residential landscape design and construction business said, "Hey, Curt. You're looking for a new gig. You're a contractor, wicked smart, and you're organized. You can make a lot of money doing this type of work. Why don't you try something different? Use your construction background and go for it."

So, I did. I worked for that company for a few years and learned a lot, literally from the ground up, starting with design. It was fun, and I enjoyed myself, feeling suitable for the first time in years. I was happy, and I was beginning to make a lot more money than ever before.

After a few years, I realized I couldn't continue working for that company; I didn't like the way they conducted business. Certain practices rubbed me the wrong way and went against my moral code. I realized I could do it better myself; I had skills in both landscaping and marketing, and confidently moved ahead.

By 2004, Natalie and I had been married for a couple of years, living in her house with her son, Corbin, who had become my son in every way. That June, I launched *Outside Living Concepts Inc.* using her spare room for my office. I've made a tremendous amount of money from that tiny space. I never looked back.

I love creating something from nothing—seeing a bare patch of desert and transforming it into a valuable and beautiful oasis for homeowners, something that enriches the lives of those who use it daily. The process satisfies my creative needs, utilizes my construction skills, and leverages my sales talent.

Let me share an example: I was hired to design landscaping for several lots in a new subdivision. I discovered a lot in this community, one with privacy and an overwhelmingly gorgeous mountain view. The day it was available for sale, I made a deposit to secure the lot and drove straight to the site with my wife, a vision for a gorgeous backyard, and a can of spray paint. I walked around in the sunshine, spray paint in hand, and in one short hour, it miraculously came to life, and oh so quickly. We built our house in 2019, and since then, 52 of my neighbors have used Outside Living Concepts for their yards, constituting the biggest showroom on earth.

My business has given me many rewards and pleasures, and for the first time, I have financial independence. I'm the only employee; I utilize subcontractors and a network of independent contractors to design and manage our work. I prefer street-smart associates to book-smart people. Someone can be a great designer, but no matter how good they are, they must successfully ask for the sale and close the deal.

In 2008, the housing market hit the skids. To survive, I decided to delve into internet marketing. My hands were shaking when I signed a long-term contract and wrote a huge check. This was another defining moment. If I hadn't committed to this shift in marketing, I would have lost my business. Instead, I never looked back, and it was the best decision I made to grow the business. We currently spend $10,000 a month on online advertising, and it's worth every penny. Spending $120,000 per year to gross $6 million? *Yes, I'll take that!*

Over the last 20 years, my company has sold more than $100 million in business. Now, all four of our kids are part of the business as designers and managers, and they've added immeasurably to the company's value. They brought us fully into the modern technological era. Now, each of my eight designers works from home using top-of-the-line software to present our clients with irresistible 3-D landscape designs. The software can do a much better job of conveying a client's vision than I ever imagined possible when I began.

Although my finger is still on the pulse, Derek, Reid, Courtney, and Corbin are involved in all the decision-making. They will acquire the business from me after December 2028, and the four of them will split the profits. I'm proud of them all. They always make good choices.

I finally got a full grasp of my strengths and weaknesses when I was building my business from scratch.

My ADHD, for example. I didn't fully understand the complete scope of what it was until I was an adult. Now I consider it a key strength and an asset. I've redirected it and rely on it daily to stay laser-focused. For those who have ADHD, channel it in a positive direction, and it can reap huge rewards.

Another key strength is my ability to design and build a simple master plan. It's an offshoot of value engineering, a concept I learned in construction and later applied to my television syndication project. Now, I create a master plan for everything I do, regardless of the task's size. It's *My Guidebook to Success.*

> " I'll never be the person who watches life go by, but instead, I jump in with both feet and all the passion that's needed. "

Don't be overwhelmed by the big picture; keep your focus by taking the task incrementally.

- Ask yourself, how will I accomplish this mission?
- Realize it won't happen overnight.
- Stick with the task at hand.
- Break it down, day by day, into baby steps.
- Eventually, you will get to the end.
- Remember, success leaves clues, so mirror the actions of other successful entrepreneurs, and you'll achieve identical results.

Was it that difficult? It looks almost too simple, but it's helpful to me every day of my life. Whether you're making straw hats or starting a landscape business, apply the entire program to every task.

I've been good at what I do. My ability to accomplish what others think can't be done is innate, but I know how to encourage others to harness their perseverance, along with passion, and show them how to follow a master plan.

Attitude is Everything! is still my motto, and it hasn't let me down yet. In the next segment of my life, I have plenty of plans, and it'll still come in handy.

Learning something new and starting a business has a unique

attraction to me. It helps keep me young and my mind nimble. Recently, I was invited to participate in a restaurant and entertainment space in Marblehead with two fantastic partners, Edgar Alleyne and Johnny Ray. It's a field that's entirely new for me, but I'm using my master plan and taking one small step at a time. Between my partners and me, we're making it an exciting and viable business. I'm enjoying every moment of my new endeavor.

Motivational speaking also appeals to me, and I plan to pursue a part-time career in that field. I'm assembling trainers and mentors who will help me assist others in reaching their goals.

I'm splitting my free time between my houses in Phoenix and Marblehead. I'm also keeping a close eye on both businesses, and I'm enjoying the challenges they present. It keeps me busy. Natalie and I are still setting aside time for international travel. Running Outside Living Concepts for its first 20 years tied us down, and we have been working diligently to make up for lost time over the last few years. We're seeing the world and enjoying every moment.

I love flying, golfing, camping, and almost anything outdoors, and it is nice to have the resources to do so. Yes, starting and building Outside Living Concepts over the last 20 years has tied us down, but I have no regrets. I'm proud of what I've done with the company, my marriage, and my family.

Natalie and I have common goals and shared values, but we're such different people. Could I have made it without her? Maybe. Would I have wanted to? Never. She's the yin to my yang. If I complain about anything right now, I'm just being selfish because I have so much. Before I realized my attitude needed adjustment thirty years ago, I would never have imagined the life I'm living now in my wildest dreams.

I'll never be the person who watches life go by, but instead, I jump in with both feet and all the passion that's needed. A mind in motion stays in motion, and so does a body in motion. Motion suits me. Until I reach the end, I'll always try to create something from nothing, and I'll keep a great attitude along the way.

ABOUT CURT HAVENS

Also known as Rensselaer Curtiss Havens III, Curt is the oldest of five children born to a hardworking family in Marblehead, Massachusetts, a small seaside community north of Boston.

His father, Rensselaer Jr. (Rens), a local contractor, and his mother, Rita, a real estate agent, taught their large family to work together as a team. Curt always had a strong work ethic. At age 10, he had a newspaper route, and he worked for his father's construction firm as soon as he was old enough to swing a hammer.

Inspired by his barnstormer grandfather, Rensselaer Curtiss Sr., one of American Airlines' first pilots, Curt used his own money to pay for ground school and flying lessons. He soloed at 16 and earned his pilot's license almost as soon as he received his driver's license.

After graduating from Arizona State University with a B.S. degree in marketing, he used his construction experience in all his entrepreneurial endeavors. He moved back to Marblehead to work in his father's construction business, flipping homes on the side. Next, he developed and hosted the first nationally syndicated DIY show, Home Improvement Magazine. In 1992, he appeared on the Oprah Winfrey Show as a guest expert.

His third career move, into landscape design and construction, incorporated both his marketing and construction skills. In a few years, he went out on his own and founded Outside Living Concepts Inc., a multi-million-dollar business. His four children, Derek, Reid, Courtney, and Corbin, now co-manage the company and will take over soon.

Curt and his wife, Natalie, have recently ventured into the hospitality field in his hometown of Marblehead, becoming partners in the Beacon Restaurant and Bar, which features two movie theaters.

He and Natalie divide their time between Phoenix, Arizona, and Marblehead, and enjoy international travel.

 Outsidelivingconcepts.com

 Curt Havens

Resilience:
The Underdog's Equalizer

SAMUEL D. BEAN, JR.

When Robert Schuller said, "Tough times never last, but tough people do," he was describing my life.

If you nurture and discipline your resilience, you can overcome adversity, reinvent yourself, and remove *the impossible* from your vocabulary. It makes it easier to begin again because you are more prepared based on the lessons you learned from past experiences. Resilience gives you a curriculum to reinvent yourself, something that a college course can't provide. The more opportunities you have to reinvent yourself, the more valuable you become to society. Integrity, resilience, and servitude are the foundation for success.

Like many self-made and first-generation millionaires, I was born into poverty. I grew up fast, which was normal in my neighborhood. I always had a hustle and did whatever I could to help make ends meet.

My father, Sam, Sr., was a plumber, and my mother, Lender, was a substitute teacher. They were two loving people who somehow could not get ahead financially. Between his plumbing job and his bootlegging hustle on the weekends, my father provided to the best of his abilities. So, while Pops was doing his thing, I was doing mine.

Unfortunately, it wasn't enough, so we had to rely on Medicaid, food stamps, Section 8 housing, and other assistance programs providing government block cheese, rice, and powdered milk. One thing is certain: They ensured we had a roof over our heads and food in our stomachs. There were even times when I went to Toys for Tots with Mom to get our Christmas presents. My mother was a sweetheart, funny, a great cook, loving, a disciplinarian, and fearless. She ensured we were clean and never missed school because education was essential to her.

One of the worst neighborhoods in Houston is the Fifth Ward. I witnessed and experienced things a child should never have to. Once, a man hit my mother and attempted to kidnap her while she was taking trash to the dumpster. I was struck by a truck in a hit-and-run incident when I was five. My forehead was busted wide open, and my leg was broken at the hip. But my spirit remained unbroken.

As the oldest of four children, I obligated myself to help the family as needed and only kept what was left for myself. I started earning money when I was just seven. I jumped into dumpsters to recycle cans and bottles. I could draw well, so I drew cartoon characters, copied illustrations from a children's picture Bible, and sold my drawings on the street corner for 50 cents or a dollar. I also illustrated t-shirts, pumped gas for coins, bought and resold candy, and started mowing lawns using a lawn mower I purchased for $25 at the junkyard. From the mowing gig, I saved money and bought multiple mowers that I rented out to my friends. As I got older, I learned to cut hair and write love letters for cash.

Our family was close, so the love, laughter, and dreams distracted me from the pain and insecurities of poverty while I was growing up. I had a healthy love and admiration for my father but an equally healthy fear of him as well. Despite the financial disappointments and occasional jail stints for bootlegging, I was always close to him. I didn't judge him as a kid because he was my hero and because it was common in our environment.

When I became a teenager, I began to resent him because I felt I was left to do his job. When I became an adult, we had a good conversation that helped me understand the generational curses he inherited along with the obstacles of his time. Now, I have a greater appreciation for his belt, which set me on the right path, and our conversations kept me on it. My childhood served as my right of passage to the life I would continue to appreciate today.

When I returned from the military, Pops said, "I'm proud of you and the man you've become. I always knew you'd be a better man than me!" I will treasure that moment for the rest of my days.

> Resilience gives you a curriculum to reinvent yourself, one that a college course can't.

A few months after graduating from high school in 1990, I enrolled in the Army. I saw it as my only chance to escape, start a new life, buy Mom a home, and earn money for college. The structure, discipline, and leadership skills I acquired would help me reinvent myself. It allowed me to see the world and interact with other nationalities for the first time. I thrived in the Army, which recognized my achievements.

I was excited about my new life until Desert Storm kicked off. I was afraid of losing my life at war overseas. I called my mother every day, and in hindsight, I regret it. I unknowingly stressed her out.

Mom died the day before my 21st birthday; it was sudden, and she was only 40 years old. She was everything to me, and now she was gone. I was devastated and felt helpless because I wasn't there to help when she passed. I was upset because I never had an opportunity to buy her a home like I'd dreamed. My grandmother took my two sisters in and did what she could, but you could tell it burdened her. As the oldest, I had to support my siblings, so I came home when I finished my tour in 1996. I just needed a moment to create some cash flow, starting from scratch.

After just one semester, I realized I had to forgo college to earn more cash, so I dropped out of Prairie View A&M. I went to real estate school, got my license, and started making some quick money with an apartment-locating company. I needed money fast, and real estate was the only thing that could give me the financial and time freedom I desired.

There was one massive problem: I didn't know anyone in the market to buy or sell a home. Remember, all my contacts were from the land of government assistance, bad credit, low income, and criminal records. My solution was to move to a thriving area of Houston and find a broker who ran ads that brought in prospects and offered training.

Real estate wasn't easy—I always did whatever was necessary, never just what was easy. I put myself in uncomfortable positions, and God's compass guided me. I was not your traditional realtor. I wore jeans, polo shirts, polo boots, and gold jewelry. I also had a gold tooth. I had horrible communication skills, but as it turned out, *connecting* was one of my strong suits. I felt inadequate because of my shortcomings, but I was genuine, and people gravitated to me. I made a conscious effort to reinvent myself. I worked tirelessly on my craft but even harder on myself. I was also determined to give hope to everyone around me.

It didn't take long to start bringing in what I thought was great money. Remember, I went from making $2,000 per month in the military to making $7,500 per month in apartment rentals and townhome sales. How I catered to my customers earned limitless referrals, and the income was lovely. I loved the freedom—no boss, no clock, no need to clock in. I wasn't afraid of hard work—I'd worked hard all my life. I was also blessed with amazing coworkers. No one could stop me but me . . . no one but the IRS, that is. That's right, I wasn't paying my taxes. I put it off for years until I started getting mail.

In 2001, I decided to pump the breaks on real estate and catch up on taxes by taking a job with American Express. I had associates who were making $300,000 in their collections division. By the second year, I earned $200,000 annually on commission alone. Not bad for a guy without a degree.

2003 was a year of significant highs and rock-bottom lows. One of the biggest highs was meeting my future wife, Kim, at work. She was different. She was bright, nurturing, exotic, and had an edge. She was the type of woman you could take home to grandma, and that's precisely what I did. We knew we were committed to each other and created a plan: We'd work our way out of AmEx, I'd return to real estate, and she would do mortgages. We both got our licenses and started building our exit strategies. Kim and I decided the first deal we'd do together would be our own home, and we bought our house in fall 2003.

Everything was excellent: a new girlfriend, a new home, no tax debt, and back into real estate. Nothing can go wrong—right? Wrong. One Sunday, Kim and I were on our motorcycles, headed to visit my grandmother. Traffic was bad, and Kim, a new rider, fell behind. I pulled over on the shoulder to wait and was immediately struck by a drunk driver who knocked me two car lengths onto the highway. When I came to, I was in excruciating pain; Kim saw it all.

God had his hands on me. I lived, but my medial collateral ligament (MCL) was torn, I had a concussion, and my knee was the size of a grapefruit. Kim nursed me back to health. I'm sure that's one of the many reasons my family loved her, especially my grandmother. That's when I knew I couldn't let her get away. So, I threw a party, I proposed, and yes, she accepted.

We invited my grandmother to join us for a private Thanksgiving dinner to pamper her. Grandma had cooked every Thanksgiving meal for our entire family for decades; this would be the first Thanksgiving she'd ever had outside her home. I picked her up, and when she arrived at our home, she said, "Your mom would be proud of you—*I'm* proud of you. I've cleaned homes for many of the mayors of Houston, and this house is bigger and nicer than most of theirs."

Grandma enjoyed her day and being catered to for a change. We all ate Kim's great meal and watched football, and she and Kim laughed and talked together. The holiday was a special moment for us all. Without words, my grandmother let us know that what we had was special. She was proud of the home and my choice of Kim. My grandmother died not long after that, but not before giving Kim her blessings, knowing I was in great hands.

While I was on the mend, American Express changed my portfolio because the rehabilitation interfered with work time. My income dropped from $200,000 to $75,000 a year. I was furious because I couldn't control anything that had happened to me. Our exit strategy looked even more inviting, and on weekends, I began picking up my real estate career faster than I'd intended.

When you're about to do something big, you will be confronted by violent opposition. The year 2003 was a doozy, and it was almost over. I was approached at a church function by a network marketer; initially, I declined to join because I just wanted to focus on real estate. He was persistent, so I joined to make him go away. But he wouldn't. I agreed to come to his event because the speaker was a millionaire, and I'd never met one before. Meeting a millionaire turned out to be a blessing and a curse.

I was blown away by his wisdom and amazed at what he said. Not only am I not easily impressed, but my seasoned philosophy is that *I don't take advice from people I wouldn't trade places with*, but I would have traded places with that guy. He spoke a language I hadn't heard before—leadership, mentorship, economics. I thought, "If he'll be my mentor for two to three years, I could build a multi-million-dollar real estate business."

My first major lesson on bartering was hearing him say, "The more results you create, the more access I will give you." Soon, I became addicted to my evolution as a businessman and a leader. By this time, Kim decided to join me in that business. We earned $9,000-$10,000 per month in residual income at our peak. Some months, overhead was $6,000-$7,000 because of events. Still, this was a huge accomplishment for us. Everything I was learning applied to every area of my life, not just to real estate.

I decided to leave my other jobs and devote myself one hundred percent to MLM, following a path that felt increasingly like my purpose.

Marriage was in the air, and after months of preparation, spirits were high. We planned to be married in Ocho Rios, Jamaica, on July 9, 2005, but Hurricane Dennis washed away our dream destination wedding. Out of the 34 guests scheduled to attend, only my best man, Mark, and his wife were able to fly in, and everyone else's flights were canceled. We were married just a day later.

> " I don't take advice from people I wouldn't trade places with. "

A year later, all my eggs in that one MLM basket cracked, and I learned a significant life lesson. Even after creating an extremely healthy residual income, we weren't as secure as we thought. We woke up one day and discovered the dismantling of our entire team. A company leader left with half of our team, bankrupting our business. Talk about a crushing blow!

The disaster brought me to a level of anger and anxiety, one I had never experienced before. We went from being very comfortable with an enviable income stream to being desperate, nearly bankrupt, and in foreclosure. We had to start over from zero, so I turned to the only thing I knew would give me a chance to save everything—high-end real estate. David Cole, a very good friend, was a broker at an excellent company and got me in the door. I had less than 40 days to raise $15,000 to keep our house. I worked from eight to faint, working the phones and marketing like crazy. It was almost miraculous, but I sold four homes in that forty-day deadline. An associate bought a house that generated an $18,000 commission.

Now, it was a race against time, and the drama almost killed me: My large deal and two others all closed on the last day of the month, the same day my money was due to save the house. But get this: All three closings were on different sides of Houston. I had to collect the money and beat the Fed Ex carrier to the title office to stop the foreclosure. I arrived 10 minutes before the office closed, and the courier walked in to pick up the packages five minutes later. If I'd arrived six minutes later, our home would have been auctioned off at the courthouse on the following Tuesday.

Now that we had some breathing room, we shifted our real estate business gears. I still wasn't in a great financial place, so we decided to sell as many houses as possible to get out of debt, pay taxes on the money we had just made and spent, and then work on our lifestyle.

At that time, there were many straw scams, bad loans, adjustable-rate mortgages, and real estate developers preying on people with excellent credit. People needed guidance through the carnage. I saw an infomercial marketing a loss mitigation and short-sell program. I saw my new vision but didn't see the money in the bank account.

The vision was genius. Step 1: Place signs offering to help people refinance, save, or sell their homes. Step 2: Charge a Loss Mitigation fee to negotiate with banks on their behalf. Step 3: List the house as a discounted Short Sale to prevent foreclosure and protect their credit. Doing that would generate immediate revenue and increase the listings in my office. Every realtor would be beating my door down for deals.

I pitched a proposed partnership to my broker, but he said no. I got a loan from a retired firefighter named Lester Landry to open my own business. In hindsight, it was oddly appropriate because my business was putting out fires in other people's lives. Lester just wanted to help me, and he gave me 30 days to pay him back with zero interest.

My new companies, ForeSight Realty, and One Less Foreclosure, were a hit. We listed 86 properties in less than six months. Keeping families in their homes and off the streets was God's work. My empathy and experiences helped me make tough deals and save many houses.

Bad things were happening to good people in that real estate market. Someone manipulated a good friend of our family into using his credit to build two homes and put renters in them. Before the year was out, both tenants had stopped paying rent, he was paying three mortgages, including his own, and was underwater on the mortgages. I arranged for two short sales before my friend lost the properties to foreclosure, saving his credit and removing the debt.

Another client, a single father of four, had inherited his mother's house. He fell on hard times and refinanced it but couldn't pay the mortgage. I found a buyer who bought the house from him and rented it back on a rent-to-own agreement. Within two years, my client got back on his feet, started a business, and bought back the house. He and his children never had to move out, and the investor profited.

In 2008, we experienced two disasters: Hurricane Ike hit us, and the markets collapsed. Like Mike Tyson said, "Everyone has a plan until they get punched in the mouth." The blow from the bubble bursting knocked out our plan because the government froze every real estate transaction. We held on, hoping the market would open up soon, but it didn't. We gave our employees severance pay, and I tried to sever my emotions from the business. $300,000 in business I had in escrow—gone. My employees—gone. My office—gone. Our financial situation—close to bankruptcy. My resilience, though, was all still in place, not bruised at all. I had faced this foe before.

I had an ace in the hole, Kim, my ride-or-die. She was pregnant with our first son, so the pressure was on us both, but we had two things: a plan and each other.

The first part of the plan is to liquidate, negotiate, and eliminate. We moved all of the office furniture into our garage, and Kim sold it online. We arranged for a forbearance on the mortgage, and I voluntarily repossessed my Yukon to free $775 per month.

I asked my mentor for a loan to tide us over. He denied the loan but offered us an opportunity. He was going to launch a coffee company and said, "If you come up with the money to start, I will work directly with you to help you out of your situation." That opportunity was our best option. We put together the money and took him up on his offer.

Our master plan called for Kim to return to work for three months, hiding her pregnancy as best she could. That would keep the lights and gas connected and food on the table and buy me time to launch the business. We took our last $400, her first paycheck, and a Pay Day loan and started the coffee business. We'd bet on us before and won, so we went all in and let it ride!

Though I didn't drink coffee and had doubts about it being enough to save everything at stake, having a mentor who'd beat foreclosure and repossession in the past before he made his millions gave me the confidence I needed to do this. I was sure we'd be fine, even if we lost some things.

In just 90 days, we avoided foreclosure, bankruptcy, and repossession. Our crucial decisions were believing in each other, listening to our mentor, and making those sacrifices.

Things were so tight at first that there were times I didn't know if we could pay all of the bills. The power company shut off our electricity once while I was away at an event in Dallas. Kim didn't want to distract me; she just lit some candles and found something else to sell to get the lights back on before I got home. She never mentioned it. She was the epitome of emotional intelligence!

Eighteen months later, we reached the rank of Diamond, and I was asked to be a speaker. I told Kim, "They hear from me all the time. It's your turn to go up there and talk." She told the story of the utility company turning off our house's lights and air conditioning when she was pregnant, and I was on the road. As she spoke, I watched the crowd's reaction. Kim's words moved everyone to tears.

In many ways, 2008 was a defining year for me because it presented another opportunity to reinvent myself. While my social communication skills were excellent, I always froze on stage and was terrified of public speaking. Once, I had an event at my home, and the speaker didn't show up; I locked myself in the bedroom rather than speaking, though there were only three people there. When Kim told me I was embarrassing her and threatened to do the presentation, I came out and did it.

> " Once you master resilience, the odds are always in your favor. "

If I was going to build something big, I needed to hire help. Katrina, my excellent speech pathologist, fixed my speech disorders. My other coach taught me public speaking. I mastered my fear by weighing the things I wanted versus the activity I was afraid of. Two examples: I was more fearful of my children growing up on welfare than I was of my fear of failure. I was more afraid of my team members admiring the way other leaders spoke than I was of public speaking itself.

My mentor advised us to keep things lean and live beneath our means. You must be patient and on purpose while you are building from scratch. Patience has always been my strength, and it sits at the core of one of my superpowers. During the next eighteen months, we made enormous sacrifices. We didn't go shopping, celebrate holidays or birthdays, take trips, or go out to eat unless it was a business event. We poured our money back into the business and invested in our team. Our strategy succeeded, and we made millions in the coffee business.

The leadership and business skills I developed over the last 20 years are my foundation for success regardless of what I do. Developing and connecting with people downline in depth is crucial for security. Duplication and retention are the key ingredients for residual income. Creating actual residual income became my calling card and economic identity.

The more residual income you have, the more freedom you have. We used that 20-year window to do the things that were important to us, like travel, spending time with the boys, and working on community projects.

Kim and I have always given back to the community, including providing food and clothing for people experiencing homelessness. I've volunteered at the U.S. Dream Academy, a program for children whose parents are or have been in prison or jail. Our nonprofit, the Foresight Foundation, will serve the same cause. The foundation will expose children to entrepreneurship programs and the newest concepts and industries, such as artificial intelligence, blockchain, Web3, and more. They'll also be able to learn Spanish.

Our two teenage sons, Major, 17, and Justice, 14, attend our events and travel with us. They listen to my podcast and attend our Masterminds. I plan for each of them to open their own company one day, and I've been preparing them since childhood.

We have never used baby talk with them; we've always had adult conversations. They witness us coach and mentor adults, and we communicate with them similarly. We speak with them about critical thinking and decision-making. We are teaching our sons to be independent leaders. I'm proud to know they have a healthy respect for us both.

When I identify their challenges, I send them a video from social media; then, we sit down and discuss what life lessons they'll learn. The indirect approach works. I keep an open dialog and let them know they can discuss anything with us. It's a very different way of raising them than Kim and I experienced.

My approach was indirect exposure instead of direct pressure. I've brought my sons to events and even on stage, had them in magazines, introduced them to successful people, and much more. Afterward, they could go back to being children. I wanted them to have the opportunity to enjoy the childhood we couldn't while we groomed them indirectly.

Ultimately, I will give them self-storage units to ensure they have companies that are easy to run, produce residual income, consistently grow in value, and are assets they can hand down to their children.

In 2019, the coffee company underwent an ownership change, and the new regime made some wholesale changes to achieve their new vision that shook the company's foundation to the core, leading to most leaders leaving. We saw the writing on the wall. We stayed qualified but chose to diversify, using our residual income and starting to invest in other places. I'm glad we did because the company illegally stopped paying the leaders who weren't visibly working the business.

When the leaders left, they left with their teams, and the company's revenue went backward. In 2021 and 2022, the active leaders were paid just a fraction of what they deserved because the company couldn't afford to pay all that was due. At one point, Kim and I were owed more than $150,000.

Over lunch with one of the owners in December 2022, I told him I would support the company, but my children were my primary focus now. A week later, he suspended our account and, the following year, found a loophole to terminate us. They stole $30,000 per month in residual income from us.

They took away what we built for years because we didn't want to be their corporate slaves.

But as I tell my success team members, "It's not what happens to you, it's who you are when it happens!" After going on a few vacations, making some investments, and spending quality time with our sons, Kim and I started game-planning our next move. I looked at a new and innovative High Ticket Business Brokerage out of California and was thoroughly impressed with their business model. Meeting owners who created a compensation plan to favor the sales force was refreshing. Salespeople can make a six-figure annual income on a part-time basis without recruiting. Their lucrative subscription model doesn't require many subscribers to build a solid residual income.

Ultimately, their contract brought me out of retirement. You own your book of business, and after losing so many years of my life's work in the last company, I wanted to ensure it never happened to anyone again. Flying to the primary office was the icing on the cake. I met the principals, who were excited to hear my ideas. Now, I'm the Vice President of Sales with a percentage of the partnership of this international corporation, and Kim serves as the Director of Operations. The principals love us, and we love them.

As a child, I dreamed of changing my life and becoming rich. In The Knight's Tale, Heath Ledger's character, William Thatcher, reminded me of myself. When he asked if a man could change his stars, his father told him, *"Yes, if he believes enough, a man can change anything."* Like me, William started out poor and dedicated his life to becoming royalty, earning respect, serving his people, and marrying a princess who adored him. Despite many difficulties, he refused to die as "nothing" but accomplished his dreams on the way to his happy ending. In many ways, *The Knight's Tale* was identical to my story.

My legacy is still being written. Through my teachings, I will impact the lives of millions of people directly and indirectly. Just know this: "If you have big, significant goals and dreams, you will be confronted by violent opposition." Resilience is a muscle that grows with every challenge you overcome. It's the superpower that took me from being an underdog to becoming a big dog. Once you master resilience, the odds are always in your favor!

ABOUT SAMUEL D. BEAN, JR.

Born and raised in the Fifth Ward, the roughest part of Houston, Texas, Samuel Bean was the uber-responsible oldest brother and sometimes a father figure for his family. At age seven, he started his entrepreneurial streak, selling drawings, recycling cans, mowing lawns, renting lawnmowers, cutting hair, and even writing love letters for other guys. His mother died the day before his 21st birthday, and he returned to Houston from the Army to help raise his youngest siblings, forgoing most of his GI Bill and college experience to support them by earning money in real estate.

He and his wife, Kim, are masters at reinventing themselves after disasters, whether on a big scale (the housing crash of 2008) or being robbed of teams, investment capital, and substantial residual income by past partners and CEOs. His subsequent ventures made him stronger, wiser, and wealthier in each case. He has been a successful leader, business owner, and investor.

Driven by the desire to help people and his innate ability to connect truly, Samuel thrived in real estate. His empathy, kindness, and personal experiences led him to found a loss mitigation company that helped many people save or sell their houses and preserve their credit in the fraught years before the housing bubble burst.

Currently, Samuel is the Vice President of Sales and partner of an international business brokerage where he mentors and develops entrepreneurs. He is establishing his own nonprofit, the Foresight Foundation, to help keep young people from being incarcerated. His learning centers will expose them to entrepreneurship programs, financial literacy, and new concepts and industries such as AI, blockchain, Web3, and future technology, as well as study Spanish and become bilingual.

Samuel and his wife Kim own the ForeSight Marketing Group. They reside in the Houston area with their teenage sons, Major and Justice Bean.

 www.Samuelbean.com

 www.wecollaborate.online

 YouTube: @TheEconomicEqualizer

 Facebook: SamuelBeanTheEconomicEqualizer

 LinkedIn: samueldbean

 TikTok: @economicequalizer

 Instagram: beansamuel/

 Threads: @beansamuel

192

Born to Shine

CANDY PRUITT

Being part of this amazing book and knowing the powerful abilities and accomplishments of my co-authors is humbling. Writing my chapter has led me to contemplation, looking inward, and prayer. I've even cried, which is unusual for me.

I'm surprised by what the writing process has made me realize: *What we offer to you boils down, in essence, to our innate mindsets.* I've always called them "superpowers."

Yes, each one of us worked hard to improve and strengthen our superpowers, and we don't ever rest on our laurels. We constantly spend our time and money to better both ourselves and those whom we coach and mentor, and this is not a short-term project. We'll be doing this self-improvement work for the rest of our lives, and every one of us started young.

Our special gifts have always been there, as long as we remember, whether or not we appreciated or used them. We've had them since birth. We also know these gifts can be shared. You can take what we offer and plant the seeds in your minds, and you can nurture and help them grow. That is what we hope you will do, and it's why we're offering you our mindset strengths and secrets.

In my case, *I want to show you how to shine.*

When you truly shine:

- People will be drawn to you.
- You believe in yourself.
- You will know without any doubt that no matter what happens to you, no matter how many times you are knocked down, you will not be afraid because you are confident everything will work out.

Believe me, shining is a major superpower.

I've done a lot of thinking about how I can share my mindset with you, how I can pass on what I've always known are the building blocks of my secret superpower, my abilities to shine and believe in myself. Some of what I have to share is counterintuitive, and some of it can be hard to adopt—but you *can* learn.

Sometimes it's not learning something new but just recognizing what is already in you. I thought I was painfully shy as a child and didn't recognize my own confidence until I was in high school.

And I'm not perfect yet. While I can interact with hundreds of people on a one-to-one basis with no jitters, no matter how intimidating they might be, I still have a bit of stage fright when you put me on a real stage. To overcome this, I'm giving more talks, and I know I will overcome my fear. Perhaps my last residual bit of childhood shyness is the reason I still prefer being behind a camera rather than in front of one, but I'm working on that, as well.

You, too, can work on overcoming any fear you have, and you, too, will shine.

The superglue that holds all of the pieces of my life and mind together is deep, calm faith. You can also call it "mental wealth," which is faith in its purest state. In my case, it's Christian faith, and it's the backbone of my earliest memories.

My parents' church invited children to come forward to sit on the floor in front of the pulpit at the beginning of the service. We'd all run up front, plop down on the carpet, and listen as the preacher talked directly to us. The preacher never talked down to us because we were kids, and we were mesmerized. I always listened with everything I had in me and *always* took him seriously. I knew he was talking to me. I was just five years old when I spoke up and asked to be baptized after an altar call that powerfully spoke to and moved me.

That was just the beginning of my period of active dedication to our church. As soon as I was old enough, I taught Sunday school and vacation Bible school, whatever classes there were. I was fifteen when my dad took over his own church as a Southern Baptist preacher; he had been studying for years, and it was a proud moment for my family. The church was always an important part of my teenage years as a preacher's kid.

Faith was in me from as early as I can remember, but it can come to you at any point in your life. You're never too old to accept the Lord into your heart. Having Him in your life becomes an irreplaceable superpower—one that becomes the foundational aspect of your mindset. You lose most, if not all, of your fear.

I can't open your heart for you. I can only speak to the truths I've learned since I took Him into my own heart. It's not something you turn to just when life gets hard, though the comfort it gives is all-encompassing. Instead, faith is something you live by every single day. It can make a mediocre day memorable. Faith turns any special day into an extrasensory feeling that warms your heart for years.

Of course, I've had setbacks, doubts, and moments where I felt completely lost for a moment or two. But every time, my faith pulled me through. I want you to know that you can shine through your own struggles, not because life is perfect, but because you trust the One who's guiding you.

If your faith is based on something else, that can work for you.

I am very aware that the world is not filled with only Christians. Just remember, it's very difficult to shine in this life without faith in something larger than yourself. I know I could not be who I am without my faith.

I listen very, very well. All my life, I've listened to others. Sitting on the floor in front of the congregation and the pastor was just the most obvious and enriching listening I did when I was a child. I never use my listening power to butt in and one-up someone. I use it to learn about that person and figure out what they said and what they meant, which are often two very different things. I learn what they really *want*. That is powerful, and it helps you in any career you choose. It's the basis of everything I do in all my work (and I have a variety of simultaneous careers).

The ability to listen is more rare than you might imagine. Most people just listen long enough to be able to break into the conversation, and that can be aggravating. There are hundreds of workshops and classes on how to be a better listener, and if you're a hard-core interrupter or find it difficult to focus, perhaps one would be worthwhile for you. But the value of listening is something I knew intuitively when I was a baby, so it can't be too complicated. Oh, it's hard, very hard to do, but it's not complicated to understand.

Here's your first lesson: Keep your mouth closed. Keep your eyes open and on the speaker. Look at their expressions, their gestures, their body language. Listen to their tone and their urgency. Nod a little bit when you agree. Smile if you really agree or enjoy what they say. Think about what they're saying, *not* how you're going to respond. *Not* about how you're going to show them why what you have to say is better than what they just said. *Not* about the red flags popping up in your brain about the discrepancies you hear.

Absolutely *not* about how wrong they are. *And I repeat: Keep your mouth closed.* You can't listen when you're talking.

Wait until they're done before you ask a question—*not* when they pause for breath. Give it a couple of beats before you say a word, just in case they're thinking of one more thing to add.

Then, when you ask a question, make it a question about something they said, not a statement, not your opinion about what they said. Don't talk about your own experience, your better example, your brother's award in their field. Don't make a challenging comment about what they said or meant. Ask a question to unlock another level of the speaker's meaning. And then keep your mouth closed and listen to their answer. Think about what they say. Don't argue in your mind.

> " Faith was
> in me from as
> early as I can
> remember "

Most people can't listen for more than 5-10 seconds (if that long) before they need to butt in. Doctors listen for 11-18 seconds before they interrupt their patients. You will stand out in the crowd and most definitely stand out in the speaker's mind when you listen without interrupting them. You'll draw their eyes and attention, and they'll want to speak to you.

A friend of mine went through victim-witness training to become a volunteer representing the county attorney, working with law enforcement for victims of serious crimes like domestic violence, robbery, and rape. She said many potential volunteers could master every aspect of the training except the listening part. Those people washed out, no matter how talented they were, no matter what else they had to offer. Being able to ***listen*** was a non-negotiable skill.

Being able to truly listen is one of the most important interpersonal skills you will ever have, and you don't have to be born with it. Once you master the art of listening, you'll never regret it.

If you're a salesperson, you already know your job is not about convincing your prospect how good your product or service is—it's about making them believe they need what you are selling. Don't you need to know what they want before you start your sales pitch?

Sales is in the title of only one of my jobs, but it's the core of each job I've had, from Executive Director to Production Manager to Realtor to Hotel Concierge to Property Manager to Personal Assistant to Sound Engineer to Telephone Sales. I excel in what I do because I listen.

Let me share a favorite quote from Mark Twain: *If we were supposed to talk more than listen, we'd have two mouths and one ear.*

People tend to behave better around me. I know this may not sound like a "superpower" in the traditional sense, and I'll admit it is harder to explain than something flashy or loud. I am not boasting at all, and there will never be a Marvel movie about what happens in my presence. But I believe this is an important part of who I am because it is rooted in faith.

When people are with me, their choices often become more thoughtful and less destructive. Something about my presence invites people to become a higher version of themselves, and their energy shifts to a positive mode.

This ability showed up early. When I was two years old, I asked my parents to stop smoking. At the time, they enjoyed Texas nightlife, going out for live music, dancing and smoking, what you would expect a young couple to enjoy. They could have brushed me off but instead they quit smoking cold turkey. Looking back, I don't see that moment as manipulation or control. I see it as me innocently exposing a truth they already knew.

As I grew older, the same pattern happened with my friends and co-workers. I was popular and a leader, but I was also genuinely innocent. Not naïve. Innocent. My friends protected that innocence, but more than that, they rose to it. When people are with me, they behave thoughtfully and well. Not because I demand it. Not because I judge them.

What matters most is that they do not avoid me because of it. Quite the opposite. They are drawn to me. They enjoy being around me. The connection is real, not performative. They are not pretending to be better people for my sake. They are simply choosing to be better while they are with me.

I don't fully understand the range of this influence, but I know it exists within the space I occupy. I believe that even temporary goodness matters. Choosing to act thoughtfully, even for a short time, can begin to rewire a mindset. One moment. One better choice. One neuron at a time. That is how real change begins.

This does not mean I am uptight or delicate. Anyone who has seen me at a Nashville Predators hockey game would tell you otherwise. Sports serve as my pressure valve, and soccer stadiums and hockey arenas are where I yell, jump, and let energy out; I'm loud, passionate, and completely unapologetic.

Even when I'm yelling at the ref, my spirit remains intact. I don't wish harm; I don't carry darkness. I bring energy, joy, and light. I've learned when you lead with light, people want to protect it. When they do so, they protect the best parts of themselves, too.

I have no fear of rejection. This is an equally important piece of my superpower. Put me in a room of people and I see them all as approachable. Nobody is intimidating. I'll walk up to anybody, listen to them for a bit, and pull them toward someone I think they should meet. I'm not afraid.

We're not talking about pumping up your arrogance quotient, nor putting on an impervious shield when you leave the house. You must be yourself, have faith in yourself, stay away from people getting themselves in trouble, prepare yourself for listening, and take a deep breath.

I'm not pushy—I listen first. I don't intrude. I go where I know I can help, participate, introduce people, and help them have a better time. My lack of fear is part of that shine that appeals to people. You can't cringe your way across the room and introduce yourself apologetically to someone. They would already be turned off. Instead, hover, *listen*, and know the moment you can join in. Sometimes the moment won't come. That's okay, too.

I can do some very specific networking, and I look for clients without embarrassment. It's not crass when you truly listen. If someone's talking about their house and how it's too small, I don't hesitate to introduce myself as a real estate agent who might help them.

You can lose the fear of rejection easily—a lot easier than you probably imagine. The confidence you have comes from faith in yourself, faith that you're doing the right thing, your ability to truly hear what others are saying and feeling, knowledge that where you are and the people you're with aren't doing nefarious work. You're in a good place, and this is your moment to shine.

I've been a lowly sound engineer working on music videos with stars, a personal assistant at conferences with billionaires, a house manager at a party with celebrities, and also a movie production manager at a meeting with well-known directors and producers—it doesn't matter. I've approached them all. They're just people, people who I perhaps can help in some way. Perhaps not. What is certain is I will do my best to find out where I might fit in. They're all there to meet others, to make deals, to effect positive change, to do things better. That's what they want! They're not at home burrowing down into hibernation.

My network expands daily, and my resources expand right along with it. Yes, I attract new clients, but I'm just being myself. *I'm listening.*

It boils down to this: I want to listen to and talk to *everyone*, I want to find out how I can help them, and I want to put them together with each other.

I know it's going to work out. This is the last piece of my superpower, what gives me most of my shine. I have an innate inner confidence, yes, but this, too, can be built up if you're born without it. It's a lot easier to build confidence than learn to listen well, in fact.

> " The ability to listen is more rare than you might imagine "

Once I've made up my mind, then my faith, my lack of fear, my ability to listen and understand what others need and are doing, and the positive environment I'm in keep me afloat and pointed in the right direction. I've made tremendous changes in my life, huge jumps without parachutes. Many moves, including out of state. New careers, going full commission without a safety net. I've always survived. Some changes weren't the right ones, but my life was still on a good path—I was learning, my son, Christian, and I kept a roof over our heads, food in the fridge, hope in our hearts, and smiles on our faces.

When Christian graduated from high school and moved into an apartment with friends, I floundered for a bit until I realized my main focus of being a single mom needed to shift dramatically. It was time for a quantum leap. And I jumped.

First, I moved back to Nashville from Franklin, the prosperous suburb we'd moved to, the one with the best school district. Now it was time to be where things are happening.

Let's get some background.

Mom, Dad, and my son Christian have been my greatest influences. Mom's relentless "gift of gab" and Dad's deep faith shaped my foundation, and I've taken those two gifts from them and applied them to everything I do. They taught me to dream big, to not limit my goals, and they did their best to keep me humble and grounded.

The only time the humility lessons didn't work was when they gave me a rusty, beat-up Ford Maverick as my first car. I appreciated the gift, but I would not drive it, though it inspired me to set a goal and work until I could buy my own car.

Christian was born when I was 23, and I raised him by myself, though my grandmother and parents were there for me when I needed them. Everything shifted in my mindset when my son came into my life. He gave me a reason to rise higher. Until he graduated from high school and was on his own, everything I did was with him in the front of my mind.

He gave me direction and purpose—though it still took years before I could align that new purpose with my actual work. Christian, too, has a superpower; he has the uncanny ability to manifest what he wants, using pure belief. It always reminds me how deep faith truly runs in our family.

I was born in Texas and lived in either North Houston or nearby Willis until I was eleven. My younger brother, Shane, and I remember moving often, but our parents didn't pull us out of our schools, even driving an hour back to our Houston school when we moved to Willis. We were very close with our relatives, which gave us another layer of security and continuity. Either an aunt or a grandmother was always close enough to create the sense of a family compound. My parents never let us think we were poor; we've always been rich with love in our family. If we struggled financially, I never knew it.

When I was eleven, Dad figured the level of crime where we lived was getting so bad that it was dangerous to walk to the mailbox, so we moved to Paris, Tennessee. We had family there, too, and long-time roots in (ironically!) tobacco farming. Again, I was close to my cousins. Dad thought he could commute two hours each way to Nashville, but the commute wasn't sustainable in the long run. After a year or so at the most, we moved to the east side of Nashville, the workingman's side, not the side of town with musicians' mansions, old plantations, and good schools. We lived in a two-bedroom duplex; Shane and I each had our own rooms and our parents slept on a pull-out bed in the living room. At the time, we felt fine about our living arrangements; we were happy and stable. What mattered was we were together and doing well.

Dad was finishing up his studies to become a Southern Baptist preacher, and he was finally given his own church when I was 15. Being the preacher's daughter was a natural fit and didn't change my life at all. I was already teaching Sunday school and vacation Bible school, living the role, and Dad's job fit right in.

The last year of high school, my best friend and I chose to be homeschooled through a new Christian school program. My friend's mother was an at-home mom, and she supervised our studies throughout our senior year. When we graduated, we learned our program wasn't accredited, so we needed to take the General Educational Development (GED) program and test in order to be accepted by any of the colleges to which we were applying, which delayed us from going to college that year.

Because I'd grown up in Nashville, I was attracted to the music industry, and I had friends in the entertainment world. My first stint in college was to study audio engineering. All of the equipment was fascinating to me, from buttons and slides to microphones and mixers—the idea that you could make music sound better and be almost as creative as the artists. That led to working on albums and music videos (and acting in a couple), and it was a great career for a few years and a lot of fun.

My work was behind-the-scenes, for the most part, but I knew quite a few celebrities. To me, they were just part of the crew, and I was never overly impressed by their fame. What mattered to me was what kind of people they were, which served me well. Not being starstruck is a good characteristic to have when you're working among people who can spot phonies or those who want to rub elbows and get selfies from a mile away.

A year after Christian was born, I went back to college and took pre-med classes. Having a child may have triggered my desire to become a pediatric surgeon, but the reality of supporting us caused me to drop my classes after a couple of years and pursue entrepreneurship. I loved the idea of doing self-improvement and also loved the travel, which was the product we sold. I honed my sales techniques and worked on perfecting my other skills. The contacts I met when I was thirty led to my dream job a dozen years later as an executive director of a multi-million-dollar organization, working in film production and publishing.

Well, my experience in film production certainly helped me get the job, too.

Let me explain. My best friend was on a competitive reality show when I was getting started in real estate. She left me a message, "Hey, my producers are looking for some production assistants (PAs)." I was hired for a pilot cooking show, which was a lot of fun to work on. As I mastered the PA responsibilities, I went for three-day stints on a variety of shows, usually just weekend jobs. I did so well on one, a producer called me from Los Angeles and put me on a movie. From that moment, I became a production manager, working on a variety of short jobs as I simultaneously worked in real estate.

Those two very different jobs crossed paths one day in the air. I was flying out to Los Angeles for a few days on a movie job while I was putting a multi-million-dollar deal together, my biggest to date. I closed the deal in mid-air, landed at the airport, drove a rental car to the Sony backlot, picked up the props for our film, and paused. I stood for a moment looking at the Hollywood Hills through the palm trees all around me, and thought, *Wow, I made it!* My mind recapped all the hard work I'd done and the struggles I'd had, and I realized I'd reached a peak. I felt fulfilled. It was more than any success; it was because I knew I was right where God wanted me to be.

There have been countless setbacks along the way—financial, emotional, and spiritual. Something always comes along to test my faith. I've fallen, but I've never stayed down. I have instead grown stronger and wiser. I always knew it'd work out in the end, maybe not how I'd originally thought, but sometimes it was something better.

> " I want to talk to everyone "

I never hesitate to reach out to my mentors, I pray, reset myself, and rise again. These failures have taught me to shine brighter after every dark moment. My shine has become deeper and richer.

As I've cycled through a variety of jobs, always working more than one at a time, I've refined my definitions of success, leadership, and faith.

When I was young, success meant just achievement, something tangible and measurable. It was deals, bigger numbers, better titles. Recognition, of course.

Now, success means peace.

As I've reached what is undeniably a level of success I'd hardly dreamed of years ago, I wake up with gratitude every day. I know I'm aligned with my purpose. I've surrounded myself with people I love and appreciate, who love me in return.

I still sleep only five hours every night, but now it's a natural function of my body. I'm not forcing myself out of bed with two separate alarm clocks. I'm not exhausted. I'm not striving, working past what I'd thought were my limits. I'm shining. I feel happy, relaxed, and fulfilled. This is the type of success I want you to be able to have. On the way to this point, remember: *It will work out.*

At the same time, there's so much more to look for in my future. I'm 43 years old—not even halfway through my life, if statistics are to be believed. It's been less than two years since I changed my focus from mothering to my career, and my career has exploded with opportunities, new titles and responsibilities, and rewarding work.

Again, I'm not just doing one job. Maybe I never will! Maybe that's not your style, and you'd prefer something a little less chaotic and challenging. Maybe you don't like to make Zoom calls when you're driving during rush hour. But for me, I'm about as happy as I can imagine.

I'm also proud. I'm proud of every time I had to start over again, because I have done it with faith. I'm proud of raising my son with love and intention. I'm proud of becoming a businesswoman who leads with purpose and authenticity. And I'm proud my shine has never dimmed.

Every comeback, every win, every moment of belief in myself and faith in God—those are my real achievements and successes.

Leadership is more complicated to define. I've learned it doesn't always look like instruction, as I thought when I was young. Sometimes it looks like presence.

And faith does not always preach; sometimes it simply shines. When you lead with light, people feel it. They protect it. And in the process, they often protect the best part of themselves, too.

I know you can learn to shine and replicate these skills. Your shine may be very different from mine, maybe even unrecognizable to me. But what matters is how it works for you.

ABOUT CANDY PRUITT

Known as Nashville Candy by her many clients and friends, Candy Pruitt has a many-faceted life: as a successful Realtor, the executive director of a multi-million-dollar media company, author, entrepreneur, and rabid sports fan. She lives life fully and with joy, enjoying every moment.

Born in Texas, Candy was raised in the greater Houston area before moving to Nashville at 11. From her middle teens, she always took on more than one job as she absorbed every bit of knowledge that came her way, from college or learning on the job. In her twenties and thirties, she worked in the music and film industries as an audio engineer, production manager, and occasional extra. At the same time, she raised her son, Christian, became an entrepreneur, and launched her career in real estate.

Candy is unafraid to talk to anyone and introduce them to someone who might help them. She credits her business and personal success to several of her innate traits, among them resilience and her exceptional ability to listen. She believes these all are learnable skills, and she shares her knowledge with her readers.

For most of her adult life, she's worked on improving her mindset. She values the role her mentors play in reaching higher potential and spends much of her time and energy mentoring and helping others.

Candy lives near her grown son, Christian, and her extended family in Nashville, Tennessee, and she travels extensively whenever she can find time. She is a woman of deep, constant faith, and knows that faith is the glue that allows all the facets of her life to shine.

 theNashvilleCandy.com

 NashvilleCandy

 NashvilleCandy

 NashvilleCandy